Dance with the Devil

The Cozy Powell Story

"I've got a pretty direct approach to life. It shows in my drumming, in everything I do. If you've got something on your mind, you say it. I like that."
Cozy Powell, 1980

Dance with the Devil

The Cozy Powell Story

Laura Shenton

WP
WYMER
PUBLISHING
Bedford, England

First published in Great Britain in 2020
by Wymer Publishing
www.wymerpublishing.co.uk
Tel: 01234 326691
Wymer Publishing is a trading name of Wymer (UK) Ltd

ISBN: 978-1-912782-33-8

Every effort has been made to trace the copyright holders of the
photographs in this book but some were unreachable. We would
be grateful if the photographers concerned would contact us.

Front cover image Gijsbert Hanekroot / Alamy Stock Photo
Typeset by Andy Bishop / 1016 Sarpsborg.

A catalogue record for this book is available from the British Library.

Contents

Preface   **7**

Chapter One: Over The Top - A Life of Fascinating Ups and Downs   9

Chapter Two: Dance With The Devil   37

Chapter Three: The Jeff Beck Group (1970–1972)   51

Chapter Four: Bedlam (1972–1973)   59

Chapter Five: Rainbow (1975–1980)   71

Chapter Six: Michael Schenker Group (1980–1982)   99

Chapter Seven: Whitesnake (1982–1985)   113

Chapter Eight: Emerson, Lake & Powell (1985–1986)   129

Chapter Nine: Black Sabbath (1988–1991, 1994–1995)   139

Chapter Ten: The Brian May Band (1991-1992, 1993-1994, 1998)   149

Chapter Eleven: Cozy Powell's Solo Projects
                Cozy Powell (1973-1974, 1979-1983, 1992)
                Cozy Powell's Hammer (1974, 1992-1993)   157

Chapter Twelve: His Legacy Lives On   169

Appendices: 199
  Bands and Personnel
  Discography
About The Author   208

Preface

I can't believe that nobody has written a biography about Cozy Powell yet! That's why I'm doing it. It's time to put his musical legacy into context. It was the single that reached number three in January 1974, 'Dance With The Devil' that was largely responsible for making Cozy Powell a household name. Equally, many people have probably heard of him as a result of his work with Rainbow, Whitesnake and/or Black Sabbath (I suppose it depends what your musical interests and tastes are but somewhere in there, there's probably going to be some kind of Deep Purple related connection).

However, listening to lots of other music from Cozy's discography, ultimately, it's a significant contribution to music. Powell did so much in terms of both session work and playing with some very high — profile bands. It is very likely that lots of people will have heard more of Cozy's work than they think they have, purely because his activity as a musician was so prominent throughout his career. It's time to get all of this information collated in biography form.

In the interests of transparency and context, as author of this book I had no affiliation with Cozy Powell and I had/have no affiliation with his associates. When Cozy passed away so tragically and so suddenly in 1998, I was just about finishing primary school. As a result of this, the content of this book is derived from extensive research fuelled by a passion for Cozy's amazing music as well as the hoarding of a range of vintage articles.

The Cozy Powell Story

If you're looking for a biography that's full of gossip and information on what Cozy's favourite food and favourite colour was, you won't find that here. Besides, there isn't actually that much about Cozy's personal life out there. It comes across that as famous as he was, he valued his private life as just that. Peter Green of Fleetwood Mac was quoted in *Classic Rock* in April 1999; "Cozy was quite a private person. More than that, he was one of the nicest blokes I ever met."

Thus, I feel it is necessary to respect that in my writing about him. As Cozy was quoted in July 1986 in *Kerrang!*; "I stopped reading the weeklies a long time ago. They're all full of politics and I prefer to read about music". It is important to do justice to the musical legacy of Cozy Powell and with that in mind, I have tried to keep speculation and rumours down to an absolute minimum. Whilst I may add my own opinion here and there in the name of being objective, essentially I feel that it is important to refer to fact as much as possible throughout my telling of Cozy's story. As a result, you're going to see a lot of quotes from vintage interviews in this book. I think that's important because there's probably going to come a time where stuff like that gets harder and harder to find. It needs to be collated because Cozy Powell's contribution to music is certainly worthy of such archiving and indeed, discussion.

It is time to tell Cozy Powell's story.

Chapter One:
Over The Top – A Life of Fascinating Ups and Downs

Cozy wasn't just known as merely a member of the band, it was his name that was proudly associated with the bands he was in. Establishing a name for yourself as a musician is hard enough but to succeed to do that as a drummer, now that's really something!

On 29th December 1947, the man who came to be known as Cozy Powell was born in Cirencester, Gloucestershire. There are conflicting sources that state his real full name (I use the term real loosely as in, what is "real" anyway). Some sources say that his birth name was Colin Trevor Flooks, others say that it was simply Colin Powell, or indeed Colin Trevor Powell. I wish so much that I could clarify this one definitively but the fact that Cozy was adopted and that he never met his birth parents is such that the scope for research on his roots is pretty limited. I guess Keith Emerson wasn't exaggerating when he said; "He was a great guy that nobody knew from whence he came. It is even sadder that Cozy didn't know where he came from either."

It is with certainty I can tell you that he was born Colin and changed his first name to Cozy though. He was quoted on the matter in March 1978 in *Sounds* upon being asked what his real name was; "Colin, Cozy's been my name for the last seventeen years, and there are two ways of answering that question. The first is that there was a drummer in the fifties called Cozy Cole, and because I joined a band in school in which everyone had a nickname, Cozy it was for me! The second way of looking at it is that if someone was trying to chat me up, I would say 'Well, you can always find out just how cozy (sic) I am.' Well, it worked fifteen years ago!"

A drummer by any other name wouldn't sound as good. By the age of fifteen, he had already worked out an impressive drum solo. As he said, the stage name "Cozy" came from the jazz drummer, Cozy Cole.

As with many post-war generation musicians in Britain, Cozy would jam along to the music on the radio and on records. His first band was called The Corals. Amazingly, Cozy never had a single drum lesson in his formative years. Despite this, after deciding as a kid that the guitar wasn't for him after having a brief go on it, by the age of sixteen he was active as a drummer for a number of local bands in Cirencester. Due to the nocturnal hours of such work, Cozy was asked to leave school because of his low attainment there. He got a job in an office and after six months, he had saved up enough money to buy his first proper drum kit which was a Premier.

Cozy's interest in drumming had already developed in grammar school, during which he had played in several bands. He said in 1995; "I had a half-decent sense of rhythm, but I didn't progress until I went to grammar school. A couple of other musicians there had started putting a group together and didn't have a drummer. Because of my riotous behaviour at school, I was told to play the cymbals — because I'd broken the drums! But they said, 'Can you play on these three tracks?' It was pretty basic, but it started from there."

By the age of seventeen, Cozy was playing as a professional drummer. Just before his birthday, he had moved to Germany with the band, The Sorcerers. Like many others around at the time, a harmony group. They were to end up spending the next three years working on the German club circuit. It wasn't ultimately reflective of the great career that Cozy was going to have but humble beginnings and all that. Cozy was quoted posthumously in April 1999 in *Classic Rock*; "We'd play for eight hours a night, which was incredibly boring. I used to back strippers, so I really saw the seedy side of life, but it was a great experience. It taught me stamina and you got to try out all sorts of different things as you played, so I really learned a lot."

After the Premier kit, Cozy began frantically saving up to buy a Ludwig kit whilst gigging in Germany. It certainly wasn't an easy task though. As he was quoted in *International Musician and Recording World* in December 1981; "Unfortunately, I had spent all the money I had saved on living because they'd really rip you off. It was a terrible situation, so I had to do a lot more gigs for another six months to get the money back to buy the kit and eventually I bought this Ludwig kit that was my pride and joy. All the fittings were Ludwig apart from the pedal which was a Premier and the cymbals were Zildjian. Paiste weren't really making cymbals for rock drummers at that stage and in those days it was all the rage to have a Ludwig kit with Zildjian cymbals so that's obviously what I wanted. It was only after I went to Switzerland with Jeff Beck in 1969 that Paiste said, would I use their cymbals that I started using them, they were really good."

Cozy was quoted in *Modern Drummer* in November 1984; "I started (drumming) at school. I joined the school band, made a lot of noise, ended up breaking the snare drum and was asked to play the cymbals instead because the cymbals were a lot harder to break. That was 1961 or 1962 in a place called Cirencester located in the West Country where I come from. I always played in local bands three or four nights a week until all hours of the morning, and I'd arrive at school late, so I was asked to leave school. I did what most musicians did at that time; I joined a band in Germany and played the circuit." (That applied to many musicians at the time, Ritchie Blackmore, who Cozy would eventually go on to work with in Rainbow in 1975, also spent a fair bit of time gigging in Germany prior to his career taking off as a founding member of Deep Purple).

In the same feature, Cozy elaborated on why it was necessary to go to Germany rather than stay in England at that time; "There was no opportunity at all, virtually, in England unless you were in a professional band and had been around for a while. The competition was so strong that you really had to go abroad if you were an amateur or an up and coming musician. Hopefully you would get better as you went on. Finally, if you had gotten the recognition, you could come back to England and do well, which is what I did. I spent three years over there."

Powell wasn't even of legal age to be travelling alone to Germany when he did it. He was only sixteen. The advantages of the relaxed border control at the time combined with sheer skill and determination on Cozy's part, one would imagine. He was quoted as he elaborated on the matter in the same feature in *Modern Drummer*; "I was able to sneak in and out without their finding out, usually in the back of a van, underneath all the amps and stuff. The guys I was playing with were eighteen and nineteen. Although sixteen these days is not a big deal, in those days it was, especially playing the nightclubs, which have calmed down a bit since then. It was quite a weird scene, but it was an education."

It comes across that Cozy was motivated by the music itself rather than the commercial element of things from a young age. In the interview with *Modern Drummer* in November 1984, he was quoted as he described the deplorable conditions he lived in whilst in Germany and how it didn't really bother him because music was the priority; "We slept four of us in a room with an old boiler in the corner and rats running around. We didn't care, we were so happy to be playing. I think we were paid between twenty-five to thirty pounds a week and we worked eight hours a night. I know it sounds like 'oh sure these guys are joking', but it's true. If you wanted to be a musician in those days, you had to do that and use the most primitive equipment. I took a little job right after I left school just to earn some money to buy a kit. As soon as I had the money, off I was. The competition was so strong and the chances of your making it were so remote that the money wasn't an issue. Even if you did make it and had a hit record, you still wouldn't get any money because so many people were getting ripped off by various managers, agents and all the sharks that were around at the time. In those days, it was just a case of loving your instrument, and you practiced, practiced and practiced. That's all I did for four years solid." What an apprenticeship!

Cozy was quoted in *Beat Instrumental* in January 1976 on how his time in Germany served him well in the long run; "A lot of kids have just missed out of serving the sort of apprenticeship that Ritchie and I went through on the continent. They were tough years but they certainly taught me a lot about how to work hard and they certainly gave me a lot of stamina which you need to be a drummer. Over there you've got to work seven days a week. Most of the bands that are big now have been through that scene. If you can learn to entertain G.I.s on leave in German bars and clubs when they're pissed out of their brains at three in the morning you can learn to entertain anybody." An extremely different world prior to the days of *The X Factor* and the like! Excuse my apparent musical snobbery there! We all have our preferences though!

As Powell was quoted in *Modern Drummer* in November 1984; "I think it's changed for the worst. A lot of the bands I've heard play, without naming names, claim to be heavy metal and all sorts of things. For a start, the kids can't play. They've maybe picked up their instruments for a couple of years and decide to form a band. Well you have to start somewhere, but then they get a little bit of success via the media and they think they can play. That is a sad thing. There are not many honest musicians in those sorts of bands. I think it's put the name heavy metal into an almost joke class. People say, 'he's in a heavy metal band, he can't play and it's just bash bash bash', most of those bands are like that. Maybe it's a bit of snobbery on my part, but I don't consider myself to be a heavy metal drummer. I might have been in a band that started to do that style, but I consider myself a hard rock drummer. The stuff I did with Rainbow was not really heavy metal. The band I'm with now, Whitesnake, is just a hard rock blues band."

Cozy continued, "Heavy metal can be something that does not require a great deal of thought. You just hit everything in sight, but I think hard rock drumming is different. You start off playing rock, which is a definitive style of playing, and you just harden it up. I think generally, heavy metal drummers are not particularly interested in how they play, it's just how much noise they can make. So if you like, it's a bit of musical snobbery. A hard rock drummer is probably a better, more tasteful player than a heavy metal drummer. I could not say I'm a tasteful player, because I'm not. Jeff Porcaro is a tasteful drummer, and you couldn't put me in the same class as him."

The Sorcerers later changed their name to Young Blood. It wasn't until Cozy came back from Germany to the UK in 1968 and, upon meeting Fairport Convention bassist, Dave Pegg on the Birmingham club scene, was advised to get involved with studio session work due to it having greater potential financially and commercially. Luckily for Powell, the music scene in England had started to pick up since.

"I came back to England in about 1968, I think I went to Germany in about 1965 and I was there for about three years.

By then, we had gone down from playing eight hours a night to just four and that was so easy. So when I went back to England, the English music scene was happening. Hendrix had come over from America, then Cream and all that sort of stuff, and I started doing some sessions. I got an "in", the session scene in England was such that you had to be "in" to get a session, you had to know somebody. I managed to wheedle my way in and a couple of people heard me and were impressed. Mickie Most was one of the producers who used me a lot on his records with various people." Cozy also teamed up with Ace Kefford from The Move to play in The Ace Kefford Stand.

Cozy's next band was Big Bertha with Denny Ball, also from The Move. Ball was quoted on his memories of Powell in *More Black Than Purple* in June 1998; "I first met Cozy on stage at a sleazy club in Frankfurt, Germany in 1967. We shook hands between his hi-hat and ride cymbals! Cozy had joined my brother's band, The Sorcerers, and I had gone to the club to hear this new drummer and to perhaps have a jam with him. He was compared at the time to Bobby Elliot of The Hollies, an influence that Cozy acknowledged throughout his career. For me, the bass player, Cozy was always a joy to work with. Like having a pulsating express train pushing you along. Cozy moved to Sutton Coldfield, a suburb near Birmingham and stayed with me, my brothers Pete and Dave and my folks. He became part of the family and his west country accent drifted towards a Brummie twang. He continued to develop his superb drumming skills. He switched bands, The Sorcerers, Young Blood, The Ace Kefford Stand, Big Bertha. One day, when we were setting up for a gig at the Belfry, I noticed Cozy struggling with another drum ('It's Mitch Mitchell's!') — Jimi Hendrix's roadie had turned up with a van full of Hendrix's gear. Dave (Ball) added a couple of Marshall cabs to his stack and Cozy borrowed the extra bass drum to augment his own.

This was the first time he ever played a double bass drum set."

After playing in a number of bands, Cozy followed the advice he had been given about doing session work. He was quoted on his approach to session work post Germany in *International Musician and Recording World* in December 1981; "In those days I'd do sessions for anybody, Jimmy Page used to do sessions for anybody, as long as they'd pay you. I worked with Mickie Most, Dick Katz and David Katz, who were fixers. They'd just ring up and tell me someone needed a drummer for this jingle or that and it would be a case of going to Olympic Studios in the morning, Trident in the afternoon and Morgan in the evening."

Prior to the session work taking off and before joining the Jeff Beck Group, Cozy had met so many other musicians who would also go on to big success. Having come from the midlands, Cozy knew Robert Plant and John Bonham before their careers had taken off. Their band was called Listen at the time. Cozy also played with Tony Joe White at the Isle of Wight Festival in August 1970, having already joined the Jeff Beck Group in the April of that year.

Powell was certainly very active and employable in the music industry, even before he was asked to be drummer for the first of many high-profile bands that he was in. Although Powell's drumming method was not centred on reading notated music, it wasn't prohibitive for him as a session musician. He was often invited back to sessions on the basis of his unique sound that pretty much happened as a result of him having his own way of doing things.

Cozy was quoted in *International Musician and Recording World* in December 1981 regarding reading music; "Yeah, I could read after a fashion, though I always refused to do sessions that had reading because most of the people that write drum music don't play drums, and you see the drum part and it's so wrong. I liked doing sessions in the end that the arranger would let me play how I wanted to play it, and that's how I got my name. I had a certain style and they'd book me if they wanted that style. Everything I do, or have done, I've more or less taught myself. If someone put an orchestra score under my nose, I couldn't do it, though maybe I could work it out given time. But I couldn't do it quick enough for a session."

Cozy was quoted in *Modern Drummer* in November 1984; "I did (enjoy doing sessions) because I was playing with all kinds of different people. I had learned the trade as far as playing the drums was concerned. I was still learning, but I had a very aggressive start if you like, so if people wanted an aggressive drummer on an album, they'd book me. If they wanted a sort of straight, ordinary thing they'd book one of the other drummers on the circuit. There were about eight of us who were doing a lot of sessions in London at that time. So I'd do three or four different sessions a day at different studios and I was making good money. Suddenly it went from nothing in Germany to a really good living. I was sort of in and out of a lot of groups in those days so I was looking for a group to join."

In the same interview, Powell was quoted as he explained his strategy for getting around not being able to read music; "I could usually manage to get through a part. If there were a lot of time changes, I would try and work out what the part was, and if I really couldn't get it I would let the band run through it while I'd be fixing a bass drum pedal ('Carry on lads, I'll be right with you!'), they'd play and I'd have a very good memory. Usually if I hear a track once I can remember it. I'd be fixing this bass drum until the end of the tune ('Sorry about that, shall we go again?') and that's the way I used to bullshit my way through sessions. I was never really dedicated enough to learn to read. There is a reason for that, because I don't think drummers should read. That may sound like a stupid statement, but you play drums from the heart. Go back to the days of Africa where people would communicate with drums. They weren't writing it all down. It was played. Drums should be felt. Drums are a rhythm thing that you can't write down. People didn't book me if they knew there was a lot of reading involved. I used to tell them, 'There's no point, I can't do your piece justice. I would prefer that you just run through the tune once on the piano or give me an idea of the structure and I'll put my own little style onto your music', which is how I got most of the stuff in the early days."

As with the success of many high-profile musicians, as well as unquestionable levels of talent, the route to success featured instances of being in the right place at the right time. Whilst Cozy was working regularly as a session drummer, there was a certain Jeff Beck Group that was crumbling at the seams. Beck was dissatisfied with the group's dynamic and the band members were all going on to do other projects (Rod Stewart and Ronnie Wood went on to form The Faces).

As a result, early in 1970, Powell was invited by Beck's manager, Peter Grant, to audition in London. Powell passed the audition easily and the result was a stint in the new line-up of the Jeff Beck Group. It was through working with Jeff Beck that Cozy met Mickie Most of RAK Records. This set the wheels in motion for Cozy's rise to fame with his single, 'Dance With The Devil'. Having become more known, Cozy went on to work with so many high-profile bands in his career including Rainbow, Michael Schenker Group, Whitesnake, ELP and Black Sabbath.

Despite having the talent and professionalism to be capable of working with so many high-profile musicians of the time, Cozy Powell was a very private person; it comes across that he often felt disillusioned with the music industry and was happier going off to do things with cars and motorbikes. There are so many interviews in which, after leaving a band, Powell was quoted on the fact that he could easily be just as happy to call it a day on the music front and go off and focus on his racing interests. There are very few instances in which Powell mentioned other things going on in his life outside of music; racing was the exception.

For instance, Cozy married Madeline Turner in Hampstead, North London in April 1973. He was quoted in *Sounds* in March 1978 regarding how he found his marriage to be unsustainable as a result of his music commitments; "My wife and I split up. 'Cos of this business. It's impossible to make a marriage work if you're touring all the time. Either you take your wife or girlfriend on the road with you all the time, which pisses off the other guys in the band, or you leave her home all the time, which pisses her off, she's imagining you're up to all sorts of debauchery you may have been up to a couple of years ago, but it's not like that anymore. Women just don't understand. Look, I'm going away for four months. I'm gonna get lonely. I'm gonna want to go to bed with someone. It's a natural thing, humans do it all the time. When I first went to the States in 1970 with the Jeff Beck Group, you'd sort of rub your hands together and think of all the chicks. But these days it's a challenge. It's a darn sight harder than it used to be. Being skinny and English just doesn't cut it now, you've got to put on a ridiculous show and come up with the goods that the kids wanna hear. So now you're thinking about grafting, the social scene is gone."

Cozy was famous in the days before the whole celebrity obsession thing had really kicked off and yet, there were still famous people who were very open about their personal life with the media. It seems that Cozy generally chose not to be.

Perhaps in him being such a private person, maybe racing was Cozy's go to subject when asked about his life beyond his music. One thing is for sure though, at various points in his music career, the fascination for racing never left him. In

Kerrang! in April 1982; "I get really pissed off when people say I'm just doing it (music) for the money. Okay, I drive a Ferrari, but I don't live in a mansion 'cos all the money I get is in that car. My love in life is a flash car. I don't dress flash and I don't go to clubs very often. It just so happens that it's the most expensive car around. But that's just tough shit! I like bikes as well and I'll buy the best bike and that's where the money goes... It's not just a flash car. It happens to be the best road car in the world, that's why I bought it. It's the closest thing I can get on the road to a racing car, 'cos that's my second love. But as soon as they see you in a Ferrari they automatically think of money, which is true. The reason I have a Ferrari is because the car happens to drive very fast, over one hundred miles per hour, there's not many cars you can throw around corners. Not that I would dream of going one hundred miles per hour in Britain — I only drive it at seventy — 'cos that's the law, you know what I mean? And we've got to stick to the law haven't we?"

Also, "I'm not making more money than I've ever made. I don't get paid badly from Michael Schenker Group — it's not a fortune by any means. I'm okay, I've got enough money to buy my racing cars that's all. I'm not bothered about investing in business or mansions in the country, which most other rock people seem to want to buy. I like my racing cars — that's my only interest in life, that and my bikes. As long as I've got enough money to keep fuel in the car and get a new set of leathers every year that's good enough for me. If I do get pissed off with the business I'll go back into racing in a small way. Being in a band is very nice for all the perks you get. The limousines... well actually I don't travel in them... a lot of people like that sort of shit... First class air travel, nice hotels but you get bored. So you have to have another interest in life. Some people like racehorses, diamonds... for me it's cars and bikes. I had an interest in (a racehorse) last year but I lost a fortune. I sold it and the fucking thing won three weeks after. I don't think me and horses are a very good proposition!"

In *Metal Hammer* in February 1988; "Yeah, I've been offered a deal to ride bikes in a racing series this year, so I'm thinking about that very seriously 'cos it's something I'd like to get back into. Racing cars is one thing but racing bikes is almost like a different league — it's like going from the first division to the fourth, you sort out the men from the boys! I'm not in any hurry. I've had a long and varied career and I've been very happy with what I've done, I've been on some great albums. So if there's nothing around, then I'll go back to racing."

"I like anything that has an element of danger, and I've always found speed to be quite a turn on, I've done all sorts of speedboat riding and water-skiing and snow-skiing as well. I'd spend all day on roller-coasters — I simply adore them! Jeff Beck was into hot rods, but I was interested in racing cars, I lived with Jeff down in Brands Hatch for a year or so, so I used to go there and dabble about. After the success of 'Dance With The Devil', I was invited to do some celebrity races and I did well at those. I took it very seriously and enrolled at the race school at Brand's Hatch."

Maybe it was the case that Cozy's focus on racing was to his advantage as a drummer and vice versa. In January 1976 in *Beat Instrumental* he was quoted; "I don't drink and I'm not into any kind of dope — which is a bit strange in the rock 'n' roll business. I did that mainly because of my driving because I just can't afford to be slowed down at all. It's obviously paid off from the drumming point of view. That's been very important to me especially as we're now doing an hour and a half set which ends up with me doing a drum solo. Any kid who wants to make it has got to be fit. He's also got to work his balls off. Another thing you've got to do is watch the other drummers. Go see as many as you can and learn all the little tricks they've got. Then, when you've learned your technique you can go about developing your own style." Whatever it takes for a person to stay on the straight and narrow, I would imagine.

There are also many instances in which Powell was very candid about how he wasn't happy with the music industry, political reasons rather than artistic ones mostly. As with what Cozy said about racing, I'll share his music industry moans here and now because I think it would do his musical legacy a disservice if each chapter finishes along the lines of "Cozy got pissed off and thought about leaving the music industry" because the fact is that he didn't; it's just something that he seemed to think about a lot. Endearing really, a) in the candour of how he was in interviews and b) because it's the people who don't have a life outside of their job (yep, even rock stars!) who probably end up being the least down to earth. In that regard, I would advocate that Cozy was as down to earth as the last album he did with Rainbow in 1979.

So of course, here are some of Cozy's gripes with the music industry. Take stock of them now because ultimately, there is so much more to Cozy Powell's musical legacy than that. In the *New Musical Express* in July 1977; "There will come a point where I knock it on the head. I figure I've got four or five years left. I've had enough of it already. I love playing music but the business end of it screws it up all the time. Ritchie's had some very nasty things said about him. There's back biting all the way along the line. I just get sick and tired of all the politics. I've had some daft deals over the last five years. If Rainbow ceased to exist, I don't think I'd have the enthusiasm to start again. The business has soured me a bit."

In the *Monsters Of Rock* 1980 tour programme; "If we ever started to stagnate, I'd turn it in. Not just this band, the whole music business. When I finish with Rainbow, I'll move into another area. I won't be coming back. The businessmen have taken over from the musicians. The guys who are interested in the quick buck are running things now. There's a lot of falseness around. The superficial smiles. The backslappers with their phony talk. I'm not very good at playing those games. I'll just walk away and let them get on with it... I still think the music world is a mess."

Also, "People really think it's glamorous, don't they? Well, the time you spend onstage is great. But the rest of it is a bore. The routine can make you edgy. Whenever possible, I drive myself from town to town. I use my BMW 1000cc motorbike, or the Ferrari. Depends on what the weather's like. If it's dry, I take the bike. I can burn up my inhibitions behind the wheel. I drive fast, whether I'm on two wheels or four. On the racetrack, I'm not frightened. In a strange way, I like to get close to danger. Maybe I've got some kind of death wish. I don't know." Admittedly, the prophetic nature of that last comment there is a bit uncomfortable!

There were various points at which Cozy had had enough of the music industry. He was not without other interests that he wanted to pursue (he was also an avid fan of Swindon Town FC). However, rather than his other interests being merely a form of Cozy having a break from music, the racing thing also featured in musical milestones of his career. When 'Dance With The Devil' reached gold disc status, Cozy was insistent that it was to be presented to him in a biker's café near Chelsea Bridge. Mickie Most was quoted in April 1999 in *Classic Rock*; "We had a cup of tea and a ham roll, and then I whipped out this disc — much to the amazement of the other drivers!"

In the same article, Bernie Marsden described what Cozy was like after purchasing his first Ferrari, "He was like a dog with four or five dicks! He rolled up in it at Keele University and it was lime green, and he couldn't wait to take you for a ride in it and proceed to frighten the crap out of you."

When asked by *Kerrang!* in April 1982 on whether if he stopped drumming, would he want to work in another area of the music business, Cozy was quoted; "No, I'd want out, totally. I'm not very proud of the music business although I'm in it. There's too many people that make a lot of money out of having no talent whatsoever. I'm talking about people like managers, not musicians. I've got a lot of respect for musicians. And I've seen quite a few ripped off something rotten. It's bound to leave its mark — especially the number of years I've been in the game. You see it come and go and I've been very fortunate to do quite well. The kids get ripped off as well. The amount of money they pay for seat prices, records, it's all got out of hand. There's too many stars in this game and it should get back to the grass roots of where it started. I've seen a lot of so called "stars" treat kids as though they're dirt. I don't believe in that old cliché: the only reason you're where you are is because the kids put you there. It's only when they start knocking you down to size they realise 'Wrong — made a mistake'. But that's me harping on." When asked in the same interview whether he thought the music industry had become too commercialised, Cozy continued; "No, I just think people are beginning to lose sense of their values a bit, a little too full of themselves." Nobody likes a moaner do they? But in all fairness, there is so much realism and authenticity in how Cozy came across here. It certainly bodes well for the consideration that he was probably a realist and thus, a very likable human being.

Cozy made his fair share of fascinating television appearances in his career. He set the world record on the BBC children's programme, *Record Breakers* for playing the most drums (four hundred!) in under one minute. (A number of online sources advocate that it was in 1991 but it was in 1986 at the time of the Emerson, Lake and Powell project.)

Other fascinating Cozy footage includes his participation in the *Comic Relief* single, 'The Stonk' with Hale and Pace, Brian May, Neil Murray, Tony Iommi and Rowan Atkinson. Powell also made TV appearances on the kids show, *Tiswas;* there are two that I know of but it wouldn't be surprising if at some point more are unearthed as in, Cozy came across as game for a laugh when making TV appearances. One of Cozy's appearances on *Tiswas* was with Robert Plant. Musically, not a lot goes on in that one; the usual Q and A type stuff that one would expect from kids TV.

Cozy's other appearance on *Tiswas* was fascinating and really demonstrative of his skills as a musician and his passion for passing his drumming knowledge down to the next generation. *Tiswas* had run a competition where viewers could send in cassette tapes of themselves playing drums. The kid who won got to have a jam session with Powell and was given free tickets to see one of Rainbow's live gigs. Cool prize! After jamming with the winner and giving him some positive feedback on his drumming, Cozy didn't seem to mind getting custard pied. I'm sure there are lots of other rock stars of the time who would have been far too busy taking themselves seriously to be game for that!

Cozy also appeared on a TV pop quiz with the unoriginal title of err... *Pop Quiz* in 1981; a laid-back panel quiz show ultimately about music. Cozy was on a team with Suzi Quatro and Roger Taylor. They played against a team consisting of Paul Jones, David Grant and Chris Neil. Cozy's team lost by a few points but they took it graciously. All good retro TV fun presented by Mike Read.

There are so many reasons as to why Powell was head and shoulders above the rest as a musician. His playing was powerful and energetic yet tasteful; he played in a way that complemented what the rest of the band was doing. As prominent as his talent was, it comes across that it was never about wanting to overshadow others, even though he felt strongly about bringing drumming to the forefront of music in terms of it getting the respect it deserves. He was quoted in *Beat Instrumental* in January 1976; "I just wanted to be at the top. Drummers are almost always hidden away at the back just pounding out a rhythm. I didn't want it to be like that. I suppose that all I'm really trying to do is help put drumming on the map. Most people are drummers if you think about it. They're always tapping away on tables and chairs; I just want drummers to be noticed."

In February 1988 in *Kerrang!*, Cozy was quoted; "I spoke to Mitch Mitchell the other day and he's doing nothing at all, just waiting for something to come along. That's two really good drummers who are doing nothing. These drum machines have really put us all out of business... when I started playing in the late sixties, there were ten sessions a week available, now there are only one or two. I think it's a great shame, because less kids are learning to play drums. They are into keyboards and guitars; it is a very sad facet of the music business... I was talking to Simon Phillips and Tony Beard who are two of our best session drummers and they are actually looking for work. In the sixties, that would be unheard of. So when people ask me what I think of machines I say we should burn the fucking lot."

Powell's drumming was definitely inspirational. As was reported in *Sounds* in May 1974; "'Dance With The Devil' brought letters from aspiring schoolboy drummers – 'The whole form banged on our desk lids with rulers to it'." That's hilarious! As anyone who has ever been sent out of class for drumming on their desk can attest to!

Cozy's passion for wanting to share the educational element of drumming with others who wanted to take up the skill is evident in how proactive he was with making appearances on such related features. He was quoted in October 1987 in

Rhythm; "I've been doing this TV programme in Germany recently called *Super Drumming* which features Louis Bellson, Pete York, myself, Simon Phillips, Ian Paice, Gerry Brown and Nippy Noya. It's all about drums — people playing a bit then talking about things like click tracks and how they got started and all that. It may well be bought by the BBC and be shown over here. There you have all different kinds of styles, different levels of technique too, but I was talking to Pete York who's a very fine technical drummer — plays every rudiment in the book, forwards, backwards and sideways. He said that he hadn't found a drummer yet who got a job through technique. It was always by his feel and the way he played with the other musicians, the sympathy if you like, which is very true. I think the reason I get the jobs I do is because I play very hard and very aggressively, but also very sympathetically at the same time. That may sound like a contradiction, but it's not meant to be."

Cozy considered John Bonham as a strong drumming influence but I advocate that Cozy went further with it in terms of the range of styles he played during his long and versatile career. In an interview with *Modern Drummer* in 1997, Cozy was quoted as he discussed the way in which taking influence from John Bonham inspired his technique; "In those days there were no mics; everything was played acoustically. I started off with The Sorcerers, a band I met in Germany in 1966, which played pop hits. Everybody did that over there. The first time I came across anybody who played with any real volume was when I saw John Bonham. The kit was kind of thrown on the stage, but he played and there was this power. When I saw him play, I thought to myself 'this is where it's going, this is what drumming is all about'. I'd been playing already for ten years at the time and thought I knew it all, but when I saw John my jaw dropped to the floor. I couldn't believe what I was hearing. It was the single most important statement made to me about drumming. When I saw John Bonham, I decided to change my style of drumming. This guy had such natural ability and aggression that I just had to emulate it. I can't say that I'd ever be as good as him... but at least I could try to be like him."

Cozy added, "In those days, drummers were desperate to be noticed. They'd sit very high. Well, that's the first thing you change. The only way to get any power is to sit low. I studied the way John sat and, if you notice, he sat low and "into" the kit. People like Carl Palmer — and I'm not trying to slag him off here — but they sit very high so they can be noticed when they take their shirt off, whereas Bonzo sat low. Literally overnight I changed my drumming style. You have choices, and I took the choice of being a more solid rock drummer. The kind of impression Bonham had made on me, I wanted to make on young kids coming up. John tuned his drums open. They'd ring a little bit and have this "snap" when he hit them hard. He hit the drums mercilessly hard. He really could demolish a drumkit, no trouble. I don't think kids will ever know what that sort of physical power is like unless they've ever witnessed it." It is evident that Cozy thought highly of Bonham.

In October 1980 in *Record Mirror*, Cozy was quoted regarding Bonham's death; "I heard the news before we (Michael Schenker Group) appeared at Hammersmith and I went on to play the best show I could. He was always underrated but he was positively the best drummer in the world. The music business will be sad without him. He was Led Zeppelin in my book. I've known him for fourteen years and few people really knew him. The fact he made it so big gave me the incentive to keep going. If you're up there John, I hope you're doing a good job."

Cozy's admiration for John Bonham was perhaps embedded in the fact that he wanted to play hard rock music. Cozy was quoted on his angle on it in *Beat Instrumental* in January 1976; "I'm not really impressed by a lot these days but, personally, I like John Bonham. There's a long gap between him and all the others as far as I'm concerned. Some people may like Carl Palmer and some may like Billy Cobham but I'm talking about rock and roll drummers and he's the best. It's not that he does much that's particularly flash, he's just always there keeping the whole thing going."

Cozy wrote a tribute to John Bonham in *Melody Maker* in October 1980; "It's always very difficult to write a piece about someone you like as a professional and a friend, when suddenly they are with you no more. Bonzo, as those people who really knew him well was a real force to be reckoned with. I don't know any one drummer who in his heart of hearts didn't have a soft spot for him. Hellraiser at times he may have been, underneath all that was a kind and generous man. First impressions, speaking as a drummer are always most vivid. I remember seeing Bonzo for the first time in 1967 when he was with Robert Plant's Band Of Joy in Birmingham. I was completely staggered by the sheer power of his playing, always keeping the beat fairly simple but occasionally letting fly with a devastating power around the kit, to return once more to the business of what drumming is all about — laying it down and no messing. As a friend I'd bump into John now and again in all sorts of out-of-the-way places, whether it be a hotel suite in LA or rehearsal studios anywhere in the world, he would always manage to find the time for a chat and a drink to discuss old times. As a fellow rock drummer he was, in my book, number one and always will be. His sound and style will never be forgotten. I have nothing but the utmost respect for John. Led Zeppelin and the music business, to whom he has given much pleasure, will miss him dearly. To his wife Pat and their two children, my deepest sympathy."

Of course, Bonham wasn't Powell's only drumming

influence; Powell made a very deliberate choice early on in his career about the style of drumming he wanted to play and this seemed to be a factor in him choosing which drummers to consider as role models for what he wanted to achieve. He was quoted in *Modern Drummer* in November 1984; "I taught myself to play. I would go and see all the other drummers who played on the circuit. I would go out to all the different clubs and watch every one of them because everybody, good or bad, has something to offer. Another drummer might do some little lick that is really good, and so I took everybody else's ideas. In the initial stage, I think everybody has to do that. I would listen to all the records. I would listen to the Buddy Rich stuff and the Louie Bellson stuff in the early days, but I didn't sit down and work out how they played. I just stole the ideas they had and the amount of power they had. I've always developed that kind of style in my playing as opposed to being a jazz player. I can play some jazz style things, but not like someone who is brought up that way. I came up the English rock way, which is completely different. And I thought I would prefer to be known as an English rock drummer, rather than trying to start to get too clever. A lot of English drummers tend to, after a certain age, get a bit snobby and start claiming they can do this and that. Without patronising, American jazz musicians are so far ahead that we haven't got a chance. In those days, the two who influenced me the most were Brian Bennett from The Shadows and Bobby Elliot from The Hollies. People would ask why I wasn't into Buddy Rich. I wanted to be the best in my field so I watched the drummers who I thought were the two top pop drummers at the time. And it was easy to see them because they were playing the circuit in England. I just watched them, listened to the way they played and just developed from there."

Cozy being influenced by John Bonham is evidenced in his playing with the double bass drum technique that he uses.

It is strongly featured on the Rainbow songs, 'Stargazer', 'Kill The King' and 'Lost In Hollywood'. Cozy's brilliance was not just from using the double bass drum technique to create a thundering excitement to the music, it was in the fact that he didn't overdo it; the technique was used to emphasise particular sections of a song and thus, as powerful and Cozy's drumming technique was, his talent was just as apparent in how he didn't cover a whole song with, as Spinal Tap would probably put it, loudness.

Cozy was quoted in *Kerrang!* in June 1983 on his reasoning for using two bass drums; "To give me more power and bottom to the sound. Normally you keep time with your left foot, but if you use two bass drums you have to keep time in your head. I've been using two bass drums for fifteen years now, so I think I've just about got the hang of it."

It was in *International Musician and Recording World* in December 1981 that Cozy was quoted on explaining the logic behind his decision to use two bass drums; "I wanted to be able to play more bass drum beats but I wanted the power. If I played three beats very fast on (one) bass drum, I couldn't get the second and the third beats as powerful as the first. It took me a year to get used to playing with two bass drums. I didn't just get two to have a big kit, which is what a lot of drummers do, I've noticed. I've obviously got the technique down by now. You've really got to start again and apply your mind to it. You've got to get used to the fact that the left foot which has been used to keep time has now got to play something. Your mental timing has got to be together before you can start using two bass drums."

As well as two bass drums, another trademark Cozy Powell technique was the use of thick heavy sticks. He was quoted in *Modern Drummer* about it in November 1984; "I use particularly thick sticks. They're more like baseball bats. I've been using them a long time now. People laugh when they see them and ask, 'how the hell do you play with these?' but it's just a matter of practice really. I like to feel something heavy when I play."

Cozy elaborated on his technique to *Modern Drummer* in 1997; "One thing I did to achieve volume is change from matched to traditional grip in my left hand. You can't get the power unless you play the orthodox style. And I changed the angle of my snare drum so it angled down towards me more so I could hit it harder and get the rimshot sound. I angled the toms in the same way so I could hit them in the centre or with a rimshot. Since I've always played two bass drums, I lowered the stool so that my legs were level with the floor for maximum power. I built the rest of the kit around that. Everything went down in height. The cymbals would be positioned so that when I hit them it would be halfway through, as if you were chopping a piece of wood and the impact would be halfway down the arc. You've got the most power at that certain point halfway down. Then I went into the gym and did a lot of work. I studied boxing, which I figured was the best thing for drummers. I got speed on the bag, and I worked out on weights, sitting on a chair moving backwards and forwards. I wanted to improve my muscles in relation to what I wanted to do as a professional drummer."

Powell was very much dedicated to his art; there was so much passion and technical consideration in his approach to drumming. It is plausible that this approach served him well throughout his career. In the *Monsters Of Rock* 1980 tour programme, Powell was quoted; "On a tour, you have to keep fit. I'm feeling good for this tour. We did two months rehearsal in LA, before coming to Europe, so I'm ready. We tend to be on the road a lot, but when we get a break, I don't like sitting around. I play football, go running, cut down trees, anything. I keep busy. I still drive when I can and that helps too. It's surprising how much strength you need in your arms and shoulders if you're going to handle a powerful car in a race. On tour I'm eating all the time. Not junk foods. I have a lot of steak and fresh salads and vegetables. Plenty of sweet tea too. Keeps up your energy."

Cozy was quoted in *Modern Drummer* in November 1984 on how he warmed up before a gig; "Just fifteen or twenty minutes of pull-ups and such to get going. You can't possibly walk on stage stiff. I walk around a lot. If you think I move around a lot now, you should see me then. I pace up and down a room, up and down stairs, just to get it all going initially and get the heart rate up a bit so when I do walk on I'm immediately energetic. I don't get stage fright anymore, I can walk onto an arena anywhere. It's not a case of being blasé and saying I don't get nervous, of course I get nervous but I psych myself up like racing drivers as they sit on the grid waiting for the green light. It's the same thing playing on stage. You walk in front of a lot of people and you have to do your job. It's a very physical job so you have to work yourself up. I have to do something with both arms and both legs to push the band, so I have to be capable of walking on and doing it. I have to be in control from the minute we start. I can't afford to let it be two or three numbers before I've got it together because I'll let the band down if I do that."

As a person who seemed capable of standing up for himself and as someone who was keen to advocate for the importance of the drummer's contribution to a band, *Modern Drummer* quoted Cozy in 1997; "The first thing, when you go into the studio, is that the engineer says, 'I hear all this ringing', and I say, 'That's the sound of the drumkit, you prick! That's the way it's supposed to sound. What you're supposed to do is get that sound down on tape.' I've had so many rows with engineers and producers over the years it's unbelievable. But if you don't have overtones, the kit's going to sound dead."

Cozy's drum kit was reflective of a drummer who had really

put a lot of thought into how to get the best sound across. It was a kit built very much to facilitate the sort of heavy drumming that he ultimately became most famous for. Although Cozy's first proper kit was a Premier one that he was able to buy from his first (and probably only!) office job, his established drum kit eventually included a red glitter finish Ludwig and a mirror finish Yamaha teamed with the twin bass drums.

As heavy as Cozy's drumming sounded, the sizes of each drum were actually pretty standard (well, you can get smaller bass drums but still). Some of his cymbals were Paiste and others were Formula. Considering how intense Powell's drumming sounded, his drum kit wasn't the biggest in terms of number of drums and their sizes; testament to what he himself was doing just with his sticks, his technique and his enthusiasm.

Cozy Powell's drumming wasn't just about power though, there was so much versatility in what he had to offer as a musician. I think the content that follows in this book will really bring that to light. More so, Cozy was always striving to be the best he could possibly be, even when he had reached heights in his career that others could only dream of. He was quoted in *Kerrang!* in April 1982; "I still don't think I've reached the top as far as my playing. I'm not by any means a top drummer but I'm getting there. I say three or four years but it might be ten. I ain't about to quit at the moment though."

By that point in his career he had already played with Jeff Beck, Ritchie Blackmore and Michael Schenker. Talk about being modest! Still though, Powell was good at what he did and he seemed to always be pushing himself to go that bit further in his drumming (it's interesting to consider how playing with so many top musicians of the time perhaps functioned as a vehicle through which Powell could really expand upon what he was capable of).

As much as Powell was candid about how he felt he had

further to go as a drummer, he was also very honest about the importance of not overdoing it in terms of practice. In December 1981 he was quoted on the matter in *International Musician and Recording World*; "I've never practiced drums, apart from when I started playing. The last eleven or twelve years I've never practiced, which is something that everyone has treated with horror, saying that if I practiced I'd be so much better. They're right, but I'd lose the aggression and I'd be like a machine. I play the best when I've been doing a lot of sessions. If I'm not working I'm too lazy... who needs to thunder away at a drum kit hours and hours a day? I'm too old for that, so I'd much rather go out and have a drink. The way I do it is go on stage a little bit rusty and have to work a little bit harder."

Neil Murray, as he was quoted in April 1999 in *Classic Rock*, advocated that anyone who remembered Cozy simply for the power of his drumming was underestimating the breadth of musical styles that Cozy was active in; "The stuff he did with Emerson, Lake and Powell was more complicated than just bash-bash-bash, and Cozy relished that challenge, the trouble is that once you get known for one particular thing, that's all people want you to do. In recent years, Cozy was possibly a little bit disenchanted with the way his career was going, but it was the same for all of us who'd been in these big bands. He was possibly a little frustrated at having to play clubs and pubs; you got the impression that he was sometimes thinking, 'Why am I not in some mega-group like Aerosmith?' But it's just the way these things work out. Cozy had had a pretty good life and he always said that he didn't want to be incapacitated or hobbling around during his later years. Sometimes it's good to go out when you're still well thought of... I got in from a gig at Ronnie Scott's with Peter Green and there was an answer phone message from Cozy. It was too late to call him back, but next morning the message lights were flashing with the news from his girlfriend. It was one of those macabre things; he'd probably passed away when I picked up his message."

In the same article, Bernie Marsden, who had once had Powell as best man at his wedding, was quoted; "If he'd had the choice, Cozy would have preferred to go out in a fast car. I suspect he'd have grown old disgracefully, and he wouldn't have wanted that. We're fortunate that he made as many great records and that we can still hear him play whenever we want to."

Cozy Powell died on 5th April 1998 in a car crash, driving his Saab 9000 on the M4 motorway near Bristol. The weather conditions were bad and he was doing one hundred and four miles per hour. He was on his phone, over the drink-drive limit and not wearing a seatbelt. At the time, he had been living in Berkshire and had been working in the studio with Peter Green of Fleetwood Mac fame.

By this point, he had been the drummer on no less than sixty-six officially released recordings. His death was a major loss to the music world. Cozy Powell was a substantial drummer, it is still rare for drummers to become a household name even today and his technique was certainly something special. As well as his own phenomenal career, he had played a prominent role in the careers of some of rock music's best. Had it not been for that tragic accident, the world can only wonder what might have been.

Chapter Two:
Dance With The Devil

The chronology of Cozy's career as a drummer doesn't start with 'Dance With The Devil'. But seeing as it was such a pivotal point in his rise to fame though, I'm going to start with this because it provides the context as in, "this is the point at which many people will have heard of him."

'Dance With The Devil' was a significant highlight in Cozy's career. Not only did it make him a household name but it was a big deal for a drummer to release a single, least of all one that did so well in the charts (it got to number three in the UK singles chart in January 1974). As was reported in February 1974 in *Disco 45*; "You don't often get single records going into the charts these days that are purely instrumental. Gone are the days, it seems, when The Shadows, Sandy Nelson, The Champs, Procol Harum or The Ventures would automatically grab a chart placing just like that. Today you can be a fine instrumental outfit but just as important, you must have a good lead vocalist to add words to the non-vocal contributions. Which is why it's been great recently to watch the progress that Cozy Powell's 'Dance With The Devil' has been making in our hit parade. For one thing, it's a rare, rare event indeed, to find a drumming disc in the charts. Not since Sandy Nelson's 'Let There Be Drums' and 'Teenbeat' can we recall there being another drummin' hit. Certainly, Cozy's record is an exciting, beat-conscious record that fully justifies its high chart position in terms of musical merit and sheer irresistible impact. Yet Cozy admits, with a grin, that he only made the record for a giggle. Which isn't bad is it? Especially for someone who isn't an overnight teeny beginner in the business. For Cozy Powell has been in the business for around ten years now, with a vast amount of experience and musical background."

In the same feature, Cozy was quoted as saying that he was pleased with the record's acceptance. He was very honest about how recording the track was not musically challenging for him; "It was a piece of cake really. It only took us half an hour to cut the record and the piece itself is based simply on Ronnie Hawkin's 'Bo Diddley'."

I listened to Ronnie Hawkin's 'Bo Diddley' based on Cozy's comments here and my initial reaction was "how on earth was 'Dance With The Devil' based on 'Bo Diddley'? They sound nothing alike (both in terms of melody and drumming rhythm)". But then it becomes easier to understand the link that Cozy referred to between the two songs from where he was quoted in December 1973 in *Melody Maker*; "Mickie called me up and asked how would I like to make a drum record. I went down to the studios and played around for half an hour, and the riff was based on Ronnie Hawkin's 'Bo Diddley', which incidentally, Jimi Hendrix also used on 'Third Stone From The Sun'. We play heavy music that the kids like, and we're not ashamed of it. I use heavy military sticks, but even manage to break them! In fact I'm thinking of getting some metal sticks." Bingo! That makes much more sense.

It would seem that Cozy used 'Bo Diddley' as a starting point for creativity; 'Dance With The Devil' is certainly not a cover of 'Bo Diddley', nor does it really quote any significant element of the track. It's fascinating to consider Cozy's creativity in terms of how he got from A to B in such a short space of time when it came to making the track that would elevate his commercial profile. It sounds like the musical side of things came very naturally to him.

'Dance With The Devil' came to be because Cozy was already active as a session musician under the RAK record label, owned by Mickie Most. Many household names were under the RAK record label and Cozy had already played on their stuff. This includes, Suzi Quatro, Donovan and Hot Chocolate. Before 'Dance With The Devil' even came to be, Cozy was unofficially considered to be RAK's in house drummer. Mickie Most was quoted in April 1999 in *Classic Rock*; "(Cozy) could play just about anything. Some may say that his drumming was just about power, but he also played on Hot Chocolate's 'Brother Louie' and that was a soul record. And he was great to have around on a session because he was always so "up"."

Notably, Cozy's reputation as a drummer most associated with hard rock and heavy metal is certainly a justified one. However, his ability as a drummer was not exclusive to just those genres. Mickie Most was good friends with Cozy. He spoke highly of him in the same interview about how they shared a passion for motorcycles; "We both loved bikes, but I could never keep up with him. I'd always have to ask him where we were going; he'd tell me and say, 'See you when you get there', and off he'd go. I'd catch up about half an hour later. That's just the way he'd always been. But beneath the brash exterior, Cozy was quite a vulnerable, sentimental guy. He was never dismissive or flash."

For some context on Mickie Most, the following feature on him and indeed RAK appeared in *Billboard* in October 1974; "British music has always been a valuable export, and Mickie most has undoubtedly been one of this country's main contributors. His creative talent, enthusiasm, drive and ability to find and launch new talent has enabled Great Britain to remain a leading international force over the years... Mickie has been a consistent contributor to Radio Luxembourg's top thirty, and throughout the years, his product has regularly been included in the best-selling charts of most territories of the world. His consistency proves to be quite amazing, and his uncanny ability to spot the commerciality of copyrights or artists, even in demo form, has been his formula for success. It is true to say that without the professional promotion men in the business, very few records would achieve the highest positions."

The feature also put the spotlight on the international success of RAK in Holland; "In Holland the success story of Mickie Most started more than ten years ago with the phenomenal success of The Animals with 'The House Of The Rising Sun'. The single was number one for many weeks in the Dutch charts. Other smash hits by The Animals that followed were 'Bring It On Home', 'We Have Got To Get Out Of This Place' and 'It's My Life'."

"Another biggy scoring heavily for Mickie Most in Holland was Herman's Hermits with 'No Milk Today' and 'Dandy'. 'No Milk' went straight to number one and stayed in the charts for five months. Another historical release, still getting a lot of attention, is the original Jeff Beck version of 'Hi Ho Silver Lining'. For two years now artists appearing under the RAK label have been released in Holland with considerable success. However, since the past half-year it is no secret that all RAK releases entered the Dutch charts. Suzi Quatro was very successful and hit our charts with 'Can The Can', '48 Crash', and 'Devil Gate Drive'. Cozy Powell had a top five single hit in Holland with 'Dance With The Devil' and 'Emma' by Hot Chocolate climbed to number three. At the beginning of the year an unknown group called Mud appeared on TV in Holland. The reactions were incredible. In just three weeks, their single, 'Dynamite' climbed to number one and stayed number one for six weeks. Their follow-up, 'Tigerfeet', stayed number one for five weeks and other smash hits by Mud in Holland were 'The Cat Crept In' and 'Rocket' which both climbed to a number two position. Not since The Beatles has such a success happened. Never before has a foreign label been so successful on singles in Holland. Nice examples are that in May there were three Mud singles in the Dutch charts, and as a demonstration of the power of the label, there were four RAK singles in the top ten charts in March in the shape of 'Dynamite', 'Tigerfeet', 'Dance With The Devil' and 'Devil Gate Drive'. The RAK label is marketed and distributed in Holland by EMI Bovema. Mickie Most is a real genius in finding songs, talent and record production. He has that rare, incredible ability to create hit recordings and hit artists. We are sure he will keep up the good work for many years to come."

The article also stated that RAK was due to receive no less than four silver discs for Suzi Quatro's achievements; 350,000 copies sold of 'Can The Can', 320,000 copies sold of '48 Crash', 275,000 copies sold of 'Daytona Demon', and 275,000 copies sold of 'Devil Gate Drive' from their German recording company. Quatro was also due a gold disc for sales of her eponymous album.

Most was quoted on how he talent spotted Cozy; "I find some acts and some find me. Cozy Powell, for instance, was with Jeff Beck when I was recording him, and he had done a lot of sessions for me over the years. So when I decided to make a drum record and a drum act, I used Cozy because he was very good and he looked right."

Although there are multiple accounts in which Cozy came across as a bit embarrassed about the commercial success of 'Dance With The Devil', it seems that this was no mistake; Mickie Most was very clever as a business man. Most was quoted in October 1974 in *Billboard*; "If they're not writers, they need writers; if they're not producers, they need producers, and if they can't promote themselves successfully, then they need promotion people. What we (RAK) try to do is offer all that. We find their material, we make the records, we promote the records, we promote their image. The price of records in Europe is more expensive than in the States, so our royalties are therefore higher, and as production goes up every day, we have to look for markets where we can get a bigger return. In the States there is such a massive return factor for the product that the stores buy on sale or return. You can sell a million in America and find that you get 500,000 back which you don't get paid for, and the losses on that cancel out the 500,000 you did sell, so you might as well have never bothered. It's very difficult in America unless you get albums to sell. That's where the big money is."

In March 1974, *Billboard* ran a feature titled, "How the Chrysalis Operation Works in America". Businessman, David Sutton, was responsible for dealing with how Chrysalis would sell music to the American market. It was a relatively new venture for the British company at the time and they were keen to team up with Mickie Most's label, RAK. Sutton was quoted in the article; "We are aggressively exploring the singles market this year. The company is now trying to build an association with Mickie Most, starting with 'Dance With The Devil' which he produced." 'Dance With The Devil' was reviewed in *Billboard* in March 1974; "The drummer of Chrysalis's English rock band, Bedlam, is featured on his own by producer, Mickie Most in a pounding instrumental novelty reminiscent of the old Sandy Nelson 'Let There Be Drums' standard. Powell first embellished his reputation as Jeff Beck Group's drummer."

During the time of the whole 'Dance With The Devil' thing, Cozy had already formed his own band, Bedlam. However, due to the success of 'Dance With The Devil', follow up singles were released as a solo project under the credit, Cozy

Powell's Hammer. A good decision considering that it was 'Dance With The Devil' that was really starting to elevate his career. Band members in Cozy Powell's Hammer were Bernie Marsden, Clive Chaman, Frank Aiello and Don Airey (Powell would go on to work with Airey when he recommended him to Ritchie Blackmore for Rainbow).

Prophetically perhaps, Cozy's next single, 'The Man In Black' got to number eighteen in May 1974. Cozy's third single was 'Na Na Na' and it featured his friend from way back and colleague from Bedlam, Frank Aiello on vocals. It got to number ten in the charts in August '74.

Cozy's profile as a musician in his own right and not just a session drummer was certainly coming to be. It is at this point that I need to recommend that the B-sides of the three singles that got Cozy's solo career going are well worth a listen. The B-side on 'Dance With The Devil' is called 'And Then There Was Skin'; I advocate that it is more technically complex from a musician's perspective. This doesn't necessarily make it better (or indeed worse) than the A-side but it is certainly worth a listen and furthermore, reflective of Cozy's capabilities as a drummer.

In Colin Hart's 2011 book, *A Hart Life,* he seems to suggest that by the time Cozy had joined Rainbow (Hart was their tour manager), he had become conscious that 'Dance With The Devil' wasn't good for his street cred. That's one of those things that only Cozy would have known so I can't comment effectively on that (was street cred even a word in those days?! 'scuse my ignorance there people!) I suppose compared to Cozy's heavier drumming work, 'Dance With The Devil' could be considered to be a bit cheesy and a bit poppy but whether or not Cozy (or indeed anyone else) was pleased with the record, there is no denying what it did for him commercially; it was certainly a pivotal point in a drumming career that would result in Cozy Powell going on to do some fantastic things (both musically and commercially).

In April 1999, *Classic Rock* referred to how Cozy was apparently quite astounded when 'Dance With The Devil' started to take off. Powell was quoted retrospectively; "I didn't think any more of it until a month later when I was asked to do *Top Of The Pops*, and it became this massive thing." That's pretty funny (and probably somewhat ironic) stuff when you consider that Cozy had probably taken other engagements in his career up to that point more seriously, at least on a musical basis. Even in the midst of a good career opportunity though, it is recalled by others that Cozy actually got into a fight behind the scenes when he went on *Top Of The Pops*. In April 1999 in *Classic Rock*, Bernie Marsden recalled, "We were at *Top Of The Pops* when somebody brought it to Cozy's attention that another of the bands had made a derogatory comment in the *Melody Maker* — it was either The Rubettes or Showaddywaddy — about how he was only a session drummer who couldn't play a note. Powell never said a word, just picked up the paper, found their dressing room, asked for the drummer and chinned him! But afterwards it was all sorted and he asked the bloke if he wanted a beer."

In the same article, Neil Murray was quoted; "Cozy was always fairly wild. He was a bit of a Jack the Lad, but in a nice way. He could never resist a practical joke, and although he had a lot of front, maybe deep down he lacked a little self-confidence. He would be driving extremely fast, and sometimes he would do things to freak you out. But he was a very safe driver. I've been driven slowly by other people and felt more in danger than when I was in a car with Cozy."

It feels a bit strange to be quoting others with regards to fights that Cozy may or may not have got into and people's opinions on Cozy's driving. The former because Cozy can't speak for himself on the matter and the latter because well, you know… Make of the quotes what you will, that's what

I'm trying to say.

As much as 'Dance With The Devil' was beginning to open a lot of doors for Cozy in his career. Even, by that point, it is evident that the drummer definitely had a strong love-hate relationship with the music business. As it was reported in June 1979 in *Melody Maker*; "With Cozy's experience of solo work several years ago, when he scored a big hit with 'Dance With The Devil', the less than satisfactory handling of that material prompted Cozy to abandon rock 'n' roll for a while, turning to his other love — motor racing. But his driving terminated nine months later when Ritchie Blackmore invited him to go out to LA for a blow with his band, which was then struggling to establish a permanent line-up."

In the same article, Cozy was quoted; "I hadn't played for almost a year and went straight off the plane into a rehearsal studio with Ritchie and Jimmy Bain. Ronnie Dio was there but he didn't sing anything, yet fortunately the three of us hit if off immediately. Ritchie told me that the job was mine if I wanted it and, after sleeping on it, I accepted. We've been together ever since." Rainbow was a massive part of Powell's drumming career. Much more on that later.

In March 1974 in *Beat Instrumental*, Cozy was featured in a very candid interview where he explained what 'Dance With The Devil' meant to him in the context of Bedlam and what he felt about the commercial element of his hit single. The article introduced him in a way that really gets across that he was established as a professional musician prior to his increasing fame on the back of the single. It was reported; "He's done seventeen tours of the States, had a band with Jeff Beck which he considers was nipped in the bud and now mans the drumkit for Bedlam. Not bad for a lad of twenty-six. He also does sessions."

The article stipulates that the only reason for the other members of Bedlam not playing on 'Dance With The Devil' was the fact that the single came about so spontaneously in the studio as a quick jam that turned into a hit. I should add here that essentially, there is no official knowledge on who else actually played on 'Dance With The Devil'; there are loads of sources on the internet that state it as fact that Suzi Quatro played bass on the song but this is not necessarily true. Quatro was quoted in June 2016 in *Rhythm*; "I may have played bass but can't be sure. Mickie did use me and my band in the studio sometimes — it was a long time ago."

It is mind blowing to think of how there must be so many famous musicians whose work as session artists has been lost in the obscurity of not having been credited for their work at the time; think of all of those Hallmark *Top Of The Pops* records! (for budget reasons, the chart songs of the day were made by session musicians rather than the original artists).

The March 1974 edition of *Beat Instrumental* offers further insight into how the track was made; "Most and Powell took over the studio for an experiment. They miked (sic) up the drums through the PA, then miked the PA rather than the typical studio trick of taping mikes (sic) on each drum. Thus they got a truly live sound, entirely different from the usual drum session sound."

It's fascinating to consider that as displeased as Cozy seemed with being considered as commercial, the actual recording process of 'Dance With The Devil' was actually quite innovative at the time. On the commercial element of things, Cozy was quoted; "then it took off and now all I get is 'Yah, ya made a commercial single!' The fact that it sold wasn't my fault... professional drummers know me and my work and what I can do. Certainly 'Dance With The Devil' is easy to play. I can, and I did, double track it, play the same exactly. Well, that's not *that* easy, but any session drummer can do it."

I don't think Powell was being humble (or indeed arrogant!)

here in his comments about how easy he found it to play 'Dance With The Devil'; the fact is that it's not a particularly complex piece to play and also, Powell never seemed reserved in talking with passion about instances where the music demanded greater technical skill from him (more on that later, particularly with regards to Rainbow and Emerson, Lake and Powell).

In the *Beat Instrumental* feature in March 1974, Cozy compared the technical demands of his different drumming projects at the time; "When I play with Bedlam, I play my way. When I play sessions, I can play as soft as anyone wants, I play what they want. We (Bedlam) do get the kids we didn't get before, who are expecting The Sweet, but they find they like us. They expect a poppy gig and find they get into us... Of course I'll do a follow-up (to 'Dance With The Devil'). I'll churn 'em out as long as people will buy 'em."

More candid Cozy there! It could be argued that Cozy was being a bit condescending about the commercial side of the music business there but fairly enough, he often seemed very frank when talking about the sort of music that he preferred to play. He seemed to come across with authenticity and I'm sure that would have been endearing to many people, both colleagues and fans. Besides, he comes across as very humble when he was quoted comparing himself to other drummers; "I've got no technique at all, none at all. Barry Morgan, Pete York, the technical drummers would just make me look silly. I'm just a gutter drummer." (Many would disagree there Mr Powell!)

Finally, the article mentions that Cozy played 'Dance With The Devil' much differently in live sets with Bedlam. If any number of bootlegs of that ever surface, I have no doubt that it would be great listening. As Cozy was quoted on his gigging days whilst with RAK in December 1981 in *International Musician and Recording World*; "We did the RAK Rocks tour with Suzi Quatro and The Arrows. That was the most unfortunate billing you've ever seen. All we did was take the piss out of everyone else and all we wanted to do was go on stage and play Billy Cobham numbers, jazz stuff, and all the kids had come along to see pop stuff. It was great, and we really enjoyed ourselves, and the band were quite successful in its little own way. But it was destined for doom because we were so determined to play the stuff we liked. That was just before I stopped playing, because I got really disillusioned with it all. Bernie (Marsden) went off to join Babe Ruth, Neil (Murray) went off to join National Health and Don (Airey) joined Colliseum. Frank (Aiello) did a few more sessions before he said he'd had enough completely, and I just said cobblers, I'm going to stop and do something totally different, which is why I took up motor racing."

There had even been plans for Powell to make a full album with RAK. He was quoted in *Sounds* in May 1974; "It's difficult to say what it's going to be like until we've actually started cutting. But we want to get a very musical album with a lot of punch, not like the pop stuff at all, very well arranged and worked out. It'll be featuring mainly the rhythm section and it's a completely new concept that Mickie's got in his head."

Powell surmised what the 'Dance With The Devil' period of his career meant to him when he was quoted in *Modern Drummer* in November 1984; "It was just a drum rhythm. I couldn't really say I wrote it. It was just something that came into my head. It was Mickie Most's idea. He said 'I've got this idea for a tune. Throw a few rhythms at me', so I just sat and played a few things. He said, 'I think we'll do it like this', he just said 'play this, try that', he did the producers job. We finished it and I thought no more about it. The next month, I noticed it at the bottom of the charts, creeping up and up and up and up. It was a very big hit over here (UK) and in America it got up to about thirty-eight. Then we had two records out after that. The next one was called 'The Man In Black' which was a sort of 'Dance With The Devil, Part II'. It did nothing in America at all, but it did quite well over here and went into the top twenty. There was another one after that called 'Na, Na, Na', which had a vocal. I had a little band called Cozy Powell's Hammer, and we did a few tours. That record was a hit as well and went into the top ten. That brief period in my life lasted about two years. Then I became so disenchanted with the music business that I realised I was not enjoying it but was becoming a product of the charts. I'd had enough, I had always been interested in driving in the competition sort of thing, so I took a year off – '74 to '75 — and went motor racing. I didn't touch a drumkit for a year."

As was reported in *Sounds* in May 1974; "It's a little ironic that Cozy's suddenly sold a million records with something he could do in his sleep after spending so long becoming a really good drummer: a little like Ilie Nastase winning a huge trophy for playing table-tennis."

It is fascinating to consider that the very period in Powell's career that facilitated him becoming a household name was the same one that made him question whether he wanted to stay in the music business at all. Luckily for everyone who appreciates Cozy's drumming though, 'Dance With The Devil' was just the beginning in the grand scheme of things, as the following chapters convey.

Chapter Three:
The Jeff Beck Group (1970–1972)

In April 1999 in *Classic Rock*, Cozy was quoted retrospectively; "Jeff Beck was god in those days.
Everywhere he played was sold out and I've never seen that kind of adulation since."

In November 1984, Cozy was quoted in *Modern Drummer* on how he auditioned for the former Yardbirds guitarist; "The big break came when Jeff Beck asked me to come down and have a play. He had a lot of drummers audition and all these other guys were rapping away at this little Hayman drumkit that was there. I brought my Ludwig kit down — the old red double bass drumkit — and set it up right in front of him. When it was my turn I thought 'I'm just going to go for it and if I don't get it at least I will have left my mark. I've got nothing to lose.' Jeff was the sort of guy who would just be standing there saying 'next', a drummer has got to be in charge of the band, so I just started one of the tunes and he put the guitar down halfway through it and said 'you've got the job'."

It was in late 1970 that Beck totally reformed the line-up of his band, the Jeff Beck Group, whilst he was still signed with RAK. The line-up was Beck on guitar, Alex Ligertwood on vocals, Max Middleton on keyboards, Clive Chaman on bass, and of course, Cozy -on drums.

By June 1971, Beck had signed a record deal with CBS and needed a new singer; CBS were not happy with the vocals on the recording that Beck presented to them. Cue the recruitment of Bobby Tench on vocals and second guitar. Tench's relatively recent recruitment to the group was such that he only had a few weeks in which to write lyrics and add his vocals to the line-up's first album, *Rough And Ready*. When the album was finished in 1971, the band toured in Finland, Holland, Switzerland and Germany. The album was released in the UK on 25th October 1971 but it wasn't released in America until February 1972.

It was on the back of this that the band then did a promotional tour of America that lasted sixteen days. The work schedule was intense considering that in January '72, the band had begun recording their second album, *Jeff Beck Group*, at TMI studios in Memphis. That album was released in the UK on 9th June 1972. A promotional tour followed that included an appearance on BBC Radio One.

By 24th July 1972, the Jeff Beck Group was announced as having officially disbanded; Beck's management issued an incredibly vague statement that broke the news and as a result, not much is known about the reasons behind the break-up. What a whirlwind! It was only years later when Cozy had become a household name that he had the platform of interviews to discuss the break-up in hindsight.

The speed with which Cozy's time with the Jeff Beck Group came and went is such that the band didn't leave behind a substantial legacy. The *Rough And Ready* album significantly underperformed compared to the two albums made by the first line-up, pre Cozy.

Rough And Ready was the first album by the Jeff Beck Group not to finish in the top twenty. A disappointing outcome considering that Beck had so much confidence in the group responsible for the album, so much so that during its recording, Beck took the risk of destroying the master tapes in order to add more to it at the last minute.

In 2014, Max Middleton was quoted in *Keyboard*; "We'd finished *Rough And Ready* and it was now time to put it in its box. Then Cozy announced to Jeff that he'd bought a brand new drum kit, it had just arrived, and he wanted to put it on the record."

As much of a risk as this was to the master tapes, Beck had faith in Cozy. As Middleton continued, "They put the tape on, and Jeff said, 'If you make a mistake, I'm gonna kill you', Cozy played the album from the beginning to the end with his new drum kit, straight up. That shows what a great drummer he was. You wouldn't have known that he'd overdubbed drums on the whole album."

There seems to be no doubt that technically and professionally, Powell was on top of his game, even though commercially he had yet to really come into his own. For Beck, Cozy must have been a good musician to work with in such regard. It's a shame that the *Rough And Ready* album didn't quite reward Beck with the commercial success that he perhaps seemed to be hoping for. It received mixed reviews. In November 1971 in *Rolling Stone*, *Rough And Ready* was reviewed; "A surprisingly fine piece of work from a man who wasn't really expected to come back. Beck is back, and in pretty good shape too." The album was also reviewed in March 1972 in *The Village Voice*; "Despite some superb textures, this is as sloppy and self-indulgent as ever."

Unlike the *Rough And Ready* album, the band's following eponymous one featured five songs that were covers including 'Glad All Over' by Carl Perkins and 'I Can't Give Back The Love I Feel For You' by Ashford and Simpson. There were no singles released from the album. Like the album before it, the *Jeff Beck Group* received mixed reviews. In June 1972 in *Rolling Stone*, it was considered; "When either Bob Tench's vocals or Max Middleton's usually pleasant but seldom arresting and never-smoothly-integrated jazz piano are basking therein, Jeff Beck Group's music is mostly just dull — commonplace and predictable."

In July 1972 in *Oz*, the album was reviewed; "Since his last album, Beck has brought in an outside producer, Steve Cropper, no less. Unlike *Rough And Ready*, this one features some real songs, like Don Nix's 'Going Down', Dylan's 'Tonight I'll Be Staying Here with You', and a couple of Motown standards. 'Going Down' cuts Nix's own version to pieces and comes near to equalling the version Stone The Crows use for their encore."

And there were such high hopes for this line-up too! In June 1971 in *Rolling Stone* it was reported; "The band cooks. It's "heavy", sure, but it's not glue-sniffing heavy, it's mostly thudding Romilar action. Cozy Powell is one of a few drummers who can use twin bass drums and not get lost in them. Max Middleton was a classical pianist student for eighteen years and this is his first venture into pop. And he doesn't use all the old stock riffs. And Jeff taps his feet as he plays, a rare sight for guitarists; it's upbeat, crystal-clear chording, then it's all a slide back into Motown Heavy."

On balance though, the same article also reports of some of the problems Beck was facing on the business side; "A growing animosity seems to be developing between Beck and his managers, RAK. Beck, unhappy with the new record contracts being drawn up, flew to America to negotiate privately with Columbia. RAK, unhappy that Beck was doing things behind their backs and having already paid for the studio time, confiscated the tapes. The last word is that Beck, now even more distraught at losing the tapes, and thinking it unpractical to lose his gang of hoodlums on RAK, is attempting to compromise by offering two per cent of the record money to Mickie Most (who, along with Peter Grant, is RAK), in return for the tapes."

Oh well, Beck's problems with RAK didn't seem to do

Cozy any harm. Just as well considering that it was RAK and indeed Mickie Most that helped Cozy Powell become a household name with 'Dance With The Devil'. As much as Cozy stated in interviews not long after leaving, that he was glad to be out of the Jeff Beck Group from both a creative and personal perspective (there's loads on that in the next chapter, trust me), at least something really good and ultimately, pivotal came out of it for Cozy in terms of his association with Mickie Most and RAK. Besides, in interviews much later down the line, Cozy spoke highly of his time in Jeff Beck Group. Perhaps with hindsight and after playing in so many other bands, Cozy's opinion changed. Who knows?

One of the Jeff Beck Group concerts was reviewed in November 1971 in *Record World*; "Complex rhythms and stunning guitar virtuosity assured the crowd that Jeff Beck had returned to the States with his reputation intact, as evidenced by his recent appearances at the Academy of Music. With a completely new band including vocalist Robert Tench behind him, Beck ran through a number of specialities, old and new. 'Going Down', Freddie King's stomper, got things off to a rocking start while oldies like 'Jeff's Boogie' and 'Morning Dew' alternated with new Beck standards like 'Situation' and 'Jody' from the guitarist's new Epic album, *Rough And Ready*. Fine solos from pianist Dave Middleton and drummer Cozy Powell supported Beck's own performances, which over the years have grown closer stylistically to those of Eric Clapton and Duane Allman. Beck's new compositions however, showed an originality that will help to re-establish quickly the vast following he had when he went into semi-retirement two years ago."

The element of Beck making a comeback to music was also strongly referred to in another review in November 1971 in *Cash Box*. The review was of one of the band's gigs at the Long Beach Auditorium; 'Sorry about the delay', mumbled ace guitarist Jeff Beck as he opened his set... 'the two-year delay', and that it had been. The last time Beck had played the area, it had been with a band including Rod Stewart, Ron Wood and Mickey Waller. Strong company indeed, the kind that demands comparison with whatever comes next. Well, Beck is back, and those looking for comparisons came out in droves. The group's new Epic album hasn't really been out long enough to have made any lasting impression: it was the "in person" Beck that the audience was to judge. They've made a wise move. Even though some of the old material remains, vocalist Bob Tench is enough of his own man to be judged as such. He's just fine. Not nearly so much of a wild man on stage as his predecessor, he's a strong interpreter of songs. And the rest of the band, drummer Cozy Powell, bassist Clive Chaman and pianist Max Middleton stand up well against just about any similarly instrumented group you care to name."

Although both reviews do recognise the value that Cozy brought to the band, the way they were written is very much Beck, Beck and more Beck isn't it; understandable considering the name of the band but it makes me really pleased that Cozy branched out on his own and made a name for himself that went beyond being known mainly among other musicians as predominantly a session musician. Also, there is nothing in this review to suggest that musically, the Jeff Beck Group was having any problems and thus, it leaves everyone still none the wiser as to why the band broke up so suddenly. Maybe it's just as well as in, Powell and his drumming talents could have easily been overlooked if he had spent more of his career being in a band that was really all about Jeff Beck.

It is unclear as to what specifically caused the Jeff Beck Group to suddenly call it a day. It sounds like there was all kinds of turbulence and to put the band's break up down to just one thing would be futile. Their management announced it with such speed and abruptness that really, it is anyone's guess. What is apparent though, is that Cozy's time with Jeff Beck was a constructive start to his career. He spoke of this in a number of interviews later down the line. In February 1988 in *Metal Hammer*, Cozy was quoted; "That was a fantastic band. I really enjoyed that. Everybody asks me about Rainbow, Whitesnake and Michael Schenker Group but they all forget to mention the Jeff Beck Group which was probably the best band of them all, for the musicianship. I've got fond memories of that band and Jeff is still playing as well as ever. Jeff Beck is the best guitarist I've ever worked with, without a doubt, he's head and shoulders above everybody else — Gary Moore and Ritchie Blackmore maybe as close seconds. But Jeff is the best and the fact that he's sitting on his arse, pouncing around with Mick Jagger, is a total waste of talent! The sooner he gets into a band again and lets everybody see how good he is, the better."

In 1997, Cozy was quoted in *Modern Drummer* as he described what joining the Jeff Beck Group meant to him as a musician; "With Jeff Beck, which was my first big gig, I wanted to show people I could play hard but have chops as well. I'd practice a four-stroke riff and go from the floor tom to the top toms and work out this kind of rolling thing."

In *Modern Drummer* in November 1984, Powell shed a tiny bit of light on what may have caused Jeff Beck to call it a day with the line-up of the Jeff Beck Group that he was involved with but ultimately, it's pretty vague stuff. Cozy was quoted; "I didn't actually leave Jeff. The whole band was fired because Jeff was going through a bit of a funny period at the time. He just desperately wanted to play with Timmy Bogert and Carmine Appice. He wanted to do that before he formed our group, but it was impossible for contractual reasons. Eventually the chance came."

Cozy was quoted in *Sounds* in January 1974 as he reflected on the idea that perhaps Beck didn't get what he wanted from the line-up that he was part of; "The critics really slagged that band, and I thought it was one of the best groups Jeff ever had – in terms of musicianship – discounting myself of course... But in the States it was a different matter. The group was just beginning to win some acclaim, I reckon we would've started to break on the next tour. We were just beginning to do the five thousand seaters. The next tour Jeff did, he got bottles thrown at him. They gave him a rough time because they wanted to see (Beck's) last group."

Beck's approach to using pop music as a vehicle for opening more doors commercially was inspirational to Cozy during the 'Dance With The Devil' days. Cozy was quoted in *Sounds* in August 1974; "I will do it (pop music) if it'll get my group on the road... Take Jeff Beck when he started. 'Hi Ho Silver Lining', 'Love Is Blue', all that stuff, then all of a sudden came the *Truth* album. That was completely different. That's the way I hope to go – that's the sort of thing I want to do."

It comes across that Powell's schedule as part of the Jeff Beck Group was, although short lived, hectic and monumental. Time for Bedlam!

Chapter Four:
Bedlam (1972–1973)

Cozy recorded 'Dance With The Devil' towards the end of his time with Bedlam. As he confessed in the interview in February 1974 in *Disco 45*, it had been difficult to break into the British market so far. Even though he seemed to insinuate that he did 'Dance With The Devil' for a bit of a laugh, he was optimistic that it would perhaps have more commercial opportunity for him than continuing with Bedlam. He wasn't wrong. Bedlam was formed in 1972. They produced one eponymous album on Chrysalis Records that was released in August 1973. Advantageously for Cozy, he was also active as a session drummer for Mickie Most at RAK. Cozy's extra-curricular drumming, outside of Bedlam, was a vital part of what would take his career to the next stage post Bedlam.

It took Cozy and guitarist, Dave Ball, quite some time to get Bedlam up and running. The motivation was there but it was the mid-sixties and a lot of post war generation musicians were trying to make it big. Dave was from a musical family in Birmingham. There were always musicians popping in and out of the house and during this time, he and Cozy were trying to get a band together. Dave's brother, Dennis Ball was quoted in *The Birmingham Post* on 17th April 1998; "Cozy came to live with us in Sutton Coldfield in 1968. All three brothers were musicians and we used to jam in the billiards room of the house in Rectory Road, all fighting for space. My late mother took it all very well and got on with all the groups. It was a wonderful place because a lot of members of bands like Black Sabbath and The Move used to come and visit. I especially remember Cozy's wife, Madeline, turning up at the house on a horse... All this time we were broke but happy."

Having eventually built a reputation, they initially called their band The Ace Kefford Stand. Musically there seemed to be no problem; they were repeatedly asked back to clubs to play gigs to appreciative audiences but commercially, things just weren't taking off. As a result, Dave left for London in 1967 where he was able to get himself a manager. He started a band called Big Bertha and asked Cozy to play on a single that the manager had succeeded to organise. That all sounds great but no, not really; there were very few pressings made and the small number of sales of the record were in Italy and Germany. As Ball was quoted in July 1973 in *Melody Maker*, "A fat lot of good when we were based in London." The band carried on for a while but seemingly, they were pretty much just going through the motions. Therefore, when Cozy received a call from Jeff Beck asking him to play in his band, the decision was a no brainer really. Bye bye Big Bertha, hello Jeff Beck.

Dave Ball joined Procol Harum. The other members, Pete and Dennis, faded into obscurity. Dave and Cozy stayed in touch because both of them were in bands that were touring America at the same time. It was very common for them to cross paths on a frequent basis. Although Ball had embraced the opportunity to play in a high-profile band, Cozy recalled that he didn't seem to be too excited about it. In July 1973 in *Melody Maker*, Cozy recalled, "I've never seen him yawn so much in my whole life."

The timing was right for Ball and Powell to work together again; Ball wasn't particularly enthralled to be in Procol Harum and Cozy was no longer working with Jeff Beck (some sources say that Beck sacked Powell, others say that Powell left because he'd had enough, either way, Cozy was now at a loose end that would emerge to be constructive in the next stage of his career).

As Ball was quoted in the same edition of *Melody Maker*, "Forming Bedlam is a thing we've wanted to do for so long. We were getting screwed up by people simply because we didn't have enough noise behind our names. It really was just a matter of time. Cozy sparked it off this time round. He telephoned me in the states and said 'listen, what are we doing screwing about in these tinpot things?' so many times we've been in touch with one another from England to the states and back and forth and one or other of us would say 'I think I'll stay and be safe'."

In the same article, Cozy was quoted, "finally, we got sick and tired of fannying about... If it works, great... but at least we've had a shot at it." It seems that both Ball and Powell were strong personalities and although it took time and deliberation to get to the point of deciding to go for it, Bedlam was formed on the basis of them having mutual respect for each other and being at a similar stage in their careers; they were both good musically but were still seeking to become more established commercially.

Despite Powell coming across as a bit sore about his time in the Jeff Beck Group, he comes across as aware and indeed pleased about what it did for his career. He was quoted in March 1974 in *Beat Instrumental*; "The kids recognise the names and they must figure if you played with Jeff Beck, you can't be that bad."

There are simply times where Cozy seemed candid in his cynicism about the music industry. In the same article he was quoted; "I think we may get stifled. I just suss we're not gonna get the breaks. English audiences are so blasé. Groups come back big from the States and everyone thinks 'where'd *you* come from?' then the band takes this 'to hell with you' attitude, 'we were playing tight with you two years ago and you didn't want to know' it's not very professional but bands are human." Yet again, Cozy was keeping it real I suppose.

It comes across that Cozy always strived to aim high in his career. Bedlam was started in America and that is where it stayed. Ball and Powell couldn't justify trying to get started with Bedlam in Britain; they were already familiar with the music scene in America and it was considered that America was more open to new musical ideas compared to the small British market at the time. Cozy was quoted in July 1973 in *Melody Maker*; "We've both been to the states so many times now that we know what it's all about. They really love to boogie, where here (Britain) kids are so stuffed shirt and giggly. In the States they'll listen to you and get off on the music if it's saying something. Look at Zeppelin, they died a death when they started here (Britain) and yet after six months in the States, kids here wanted to hear them because they were hip. When Zeppelin started they were slagged off left right and centre yet they stood their ground and now they're the biggest group in the world. I'm not saying we're going to be as big as Cream or Zeppelin, but we're going to have a bloody good try."

Cozy continued, "The same thing happened with Cream — I know we're going to get a lot of slagging by people as Cream copyists — but they happened because they did what they wanted to do. A lot of people ain't going to like what we're doing but I know we're filling a wide gap left by bad pop music. The reaction to our gigs from audiences so far has been really good."

Cozy's determination here is fantastic to observe. It very much comes across that he was of a mindset of knowing what he was about musically and professionally; such kind of honesty and authenticity was to stay with him throughout his career. His attitude probably served him well professionally considering how many egos he would go on to work with. With Dave Ball and Bedlam, it comes across that everyone was on the same page in terms of sharing a belief that seemed to say, "here's my music, I believe in it, take it or leave it."

Ball was quoted in the same article; "I look across the stage at Cozy and Den (Ball) and I think they've got a chance to put something across without people saying 'yeah, he's a nice player but he's a bit like Hendrix' or whatever. Guitarists have got a really hard time because they've been used and used and used. You can't come up with a new lick, Django played them all before people even realised he had. All I can do is put my character across, so someone plays faster, so what, I can run up the stairs pretty fast! It's got to be your own feeling and that's something I can't put into words without them sounding like a terrible statement."

Ball added, "Guitar playing is my job, it's the only thing I can do, and all I can really do is please myself. As far as the public's concerned they can only be in tune with me to appreciate what's happening. I just play with as much feeling as I can."

It seems that despite the lack of commercial success with Bedlam, it was a key necessity in Cozy's career in terms of how, regarding the philosophy that was embraced about music and the business overall, it was perhaps a statement of intent that would stay with Cozy in all of his projects that followed.

Not being commercially successful with Bedlam was probably not the worst thing to have come out of Cozy's time in the band. His comments, as quoted in July 1973 in *Melody Maker*, are suggestive of a musician who was not easily intimidated by the bitchy side of the music industry and the aspect of it that values money above creativity. Time for just one more Cozy quote from the same article because it is just so demonstrative of what he stood for from such an early point in his career; "We want to put back some of the guts that seems to have got lost in music today. It's all gone. Have you heard any new bands with anything in the way of punch? Think back to the days of the early Who and The Small Faces and there was so much balls in their music. Turn on the radio now and it's all jeeny jeeny jink. There's no thunderous music that gets you in the guts, and quite simply that's what we're out to do... we've both worked in bands where someone else called the tune and with this band we call it. We call the tune above everybody else — above the record company, management, everybody. If we want to do something then no one's going to stop us. It's the only way to get recognition for what you actually are, you've got to do what you want. Too many musicians are influenced by other people. Honestly, I'm sick and tired of being told what to do."

Cozy was quoted in March 1974 in *Beat Instrumental*; "I just enjoy playing, it helps my musical career but I'm damned if I'm going to slog myself to superstar death just for some geezer to make money. You can be stubborn up to a point... I'd rather break this band up than go commercial, even if that meant making the money so I could do exactly what I want. I won't prostitute it, it won't change for some business man's whim."

I think it's important to add here that the term "commercial" is very relative in terms of how Cozy refers to it in the *Melody Maker* interview as in, the interviewer described Cozy's home at the time in Berkshire Downs; a newly laid turf lawn with Cozy's E-Type Jaguar parked nearby. It seems that Cozy's passion for motors was never too far from visibility, the interviewer (Mark Plummer) also mentions the model racing cars on display on top of Cozy's colour TV set. Work hard, play hard and all that. It is certainly the case that although Bedlam weren't a high-profile band, they weren't invisible either.

It was announced in May 1974 in *Cash Box* that "Bedlam

featuring Cozy Powell" would appear on the NBC TV show, *The Midnight Special* on 3rd May. I wonder how Cozy would have felt about the band being described as featuring him? I say this based on how there are so many instances where in interviews, Cozy seemed keen to advocate for the importance of a band working as a collective of equally valued musicians. The extent to which Bedlam were appreciated musically was discussed in March 1974 in *Beat Instrumental*. It advocated that Bedlam was a jam band; "All members have been keen to play with each other, to play the sort of music they choose. In fact, they've done so much session work together they feel they know individual styles and intricacies so well enough not to rehearse much. Sometimes this makes for staleness, sometimes not." The article also stipulates that vocalist Frank Aiello was recruited to the band as a result of his session work and appearance in the musical, *Hair*. There was also an unfounded rumour doing the rounds at the time that Deep Purple had their eye on him.

The *Beat Instrumental* article elaborates on Cozy's role as a leader in the band, particularly when Bedlam are on stage; "Cozy calls Bedlam's cues. He knows when Ball or Aiello are due for solos, they nod when they've had enough. He's the heartbeat and only listens to himself, his monitors are trained on him. He admits it could be hard but it's easy for him because he's always done it like that and it's easier if the drummer calls the tune because he's pushing the rhythm. He confesses an exceptionally good memory for cues. Most importantly he believes a gig is a show, an entertainment. Firstly the drummer should drive the band, shove them. Secondly, he should be visual and straight from the gut."

Cozy was quoted as he explained the concept further; "I hit hard because I think it's how it should be, power, from the heart, *feel*. Pete Townsend hammers his guitar 'til his fingers bleed so I hit hard and heavy to get it across to people. Not like say, Jon Hiseman. He's a brilliant technician but he doesn't play from the heart."

There's so much passion that comes across in what Cozy said here. He also explained the reasoning behind how he prepared for live gigs with Bedlam; "We're playing the music a lot of people want to do but daren't. We want to prove heavy music isn't dead! I know exactly where and what I'm hitting. I just hit it *hard*... some evenings we play a blinder, sometimes it's rubbish. I tend to work something out live — I never practice at home. Not even a pair of sticks. If it works live, the *feel's* there, it's great. If not, you soon know."

It is clear that Powell was very much on top of his game in terms of showmanship by the time he was in Bedlam. In March 1974, *Beat Instrumental* reported; "He (Powell) wishes Dave Ball would move around the stage more and become another visual focus. Technically he tapes his fingers because they blister and wears those black, studded wristbands for support. He desperately needs to keep his wrists tight. His style and speed are all in his wrists. He even holds his left stick sideways for the speed and he rarely uses his arms unless he's being flashy, rolling around the kit. He loves those shiny studs because they catch the light and sparkle. Hidden behind the drums he hopes, 'at least they can see me 'ands.' To this end, he's perfected a stick-toss, all part of the show."

In the same article, Cozy was quoted on how he considered that taking drum lessons can be detrimental as in, "if you take lessons, you end up copying your tutor." An interesting point and not one that everyone will agree with but evidently, it worked for Cozy and he made his drumming very much his own. Besides, in the same article he explained how he strongly believed in watching and listening to other drummers who he admired. He listed John Bonham and Billy Cobham as sources of inspiration. Cozy came across as very unorthodox in his approach to practicing. He is quoted in the article; "I'm the exception to the rule. I'm the one drummer who doesn't believe in practice... be yourself, the best way to discover is on stage." He makes it sound so easy! I guess it perhaps was for him. That's talent for you.

In April 1973, *Record World*, introduced Cozy Powell as being in a band called Beast. Beast had exactly the same members as Bedlam. My first impression of the article was that either a) there's another band that Cozy was in that isn't well known about (a plausible theory considering how many bands he was in throughout his career) or b) the reporter was talking a load of nonsense. Nope! It turns out that Cozy was in a band called Beast but here's the thing: Beast had to change their name for a very particular reason as explained in an article published in May 1973 in *Cash Box*; "From Beast to Bedlam! It has been announced by Derek Sutton, director of US operations for Chrysalis Records that the four-man British band, Beast, has changed their name to Bedlam. Acting for a Kansas City group with the same name, the American Federation of Musicians refused to allow the English Beast to enter the country unless they changed their name. The group's debut album is scheduled for July release on Chrysalis, distributed by Warner Brothers."

Both cool names for a band really. Bedlam has a bit of an edge to it though, as did their music. A performance of theirs was reviewed in *Sounds* in September 1973; "Bedlam, already guaranteed a lucrative autumn in colleges and clubs, were infinitely better at the Marquee than they had been in their introduction to journalists at La Valbonne Club a month earlier. The nature of the reception, plush club, swimming pool and bathing mermaids was totally out of character with a raw, thunderous music, lacking finesse but looking for freedom. With Cozy Powell and Dave Ball at the helm, Bedlam have managed to combine decibels with dynamics and one can now see Felix Pappalardi's interest in becoming involved with the band. Probably Bedlam played too many of their trump cards too early at the Marquee last week. Perhaps, too, they could have balanced out more light and shade with the inclusion of the popular 'Sweet Sister Mary' or 'Looking Through Loves Eyes', but nevertheless those with a built in aversion to volume were soon to be surprised. Lead singer Frankie Aiello, who occupies a stance not unlike Joe Cocker, is a veritable figurehead, singing powerfully and aggressively, grimacing and gesticulating as he spits out lyrics that become totally insignificant. But the chord themes are powerful and by the time the band had completed 'Believe In You', 'Hot Lips', with some good wah wah work from Dave Ball, 'Sarah' which concluded with a mighty drum solo from Cozy Powell, who then led the band straight into 'Seven Long Years', I was finally convinced that Bedlam have an assured future. The lengthier numbers like 'The Fool', heavily structured round 'Smokestack Lightnin'' and 'The Beast', perhaps contain a few too many platitudes to sustain interest and justify such volume. But they earned the band an encore and back they came to feature another number from their recent album, this time 'Set Me Free'. Any band that centres around the work of an old Procol guitarist, Beck drummer and Cream producer can't be all bad and Bedlam already know the secret of unleashing dynamism in direct proportion to decibels. They'll be around a long time."

Bedlam's eponymous and only album was well received musically. It's just that commercially, it wasn't on par with 'Dance With The Devil'. *Cash Box* reviewed the Bedlam album in August 1973; "The name of this band and the title of their debut LP are appropriate enough, for that's what is going to break loose once people begin seeing and hearing these very tight British rock and bloozers (sic). Bedlam is possibly the strongest band to come forth from England this year and listening to such tracks as 'Hot Lips', 'The Beast' and 'My Sister Mary' proves that substantially. No chaos here, just good rockin' and need we ask for more?"

Record World reviewed it in August 1973; "Dave Ball from Procol Harum and Cozy Powell from Jeff Beck's group are the guts of this rip-roaring powerhouse of a band. The sound is a successful attempt to "put the meat back into music" and some of the best cuts are 'I Believe In You', 'Sarah' and 'Whiskey And Wine'." Two great reviews.

And Bedlam's downfall commercially? Well, as Cozy was quoted in *Sounds* in May 1974; "What with the vinyl shortage and all that, Chrysalis had dropped a lot of acts, and because our first album hadn't sold a million, they decided that the gig wasn't going to make it, for some unknown reason." What a shame! Especially so, considering that Bedlam had done well on a tour of the States with Black Sabbath.

Cozy's drumming on the Bedlam album is indeed beautifully heavy. Is it of course subject to opinion but his drumming sounds more technically complex than that which features on 'Dance With The Devil'. The fantastic thing about listening to the Bedlam album is that it is demonstrative of the heaviness that Powell was yet to bring to one of his most iconic drumming tracks; Rainbow's 'Stargazer'.

Chapter Five:
Rainbow (1975–1980)

There was a period in 1975 when Cozy was in between music jobs. He had just finished with Cozy Powell's Hammer (for the time being anyway) and Rainbow was busy working on their first album, *Ritchie Blackmore's Rainbow*. In a number of interviews, Cozy often seemed very forward in voicing his frustrations with the music industry and being just about ready to call it a day. With such conviction, it was during this time that Cozy was on sabbatical from music and his focus was directed towards becoming a Formula Three racing driver. At the time he was sponsored by Hitachi and was racing RX3 Mazda Saloon cars.

Whilst Cozy was embracing motor racing over and above his music during 1975, he raced on nearly every circuit in the UK whilst being sponsored by Hitachi. Briefly after this, Cozy was with a group called Strange Brew with Clem Clempson and Greg Ridley but the band failed to make its mark. As Powell summarised when he was quoted in *Modern Drummer* in November 1984; "I was in six groups between Jeff (Beck) and Rainbow. One was called Bedlam which came to the states for a very brief tour with Black Sabbath. There was another one called Big Bertha, and another one called Strange Brew, which never actually played. Then I did a drum single, which took half and hour to do, in 1973. That was quite fun. It was called 'Dance With The Devil' and I think it was in the top forty in just about every country in the world."

When Ritchie Blackmore had invited him to join Rainbow, Powell's acceptance of the job was seemingly based on a financial decision. As he was quoted retrospectively in April 1999 in *Classic Rock*, "He'd (Ritchie Blackmore) seen me with Beck at the Roundhouse. I didn't have enough money to follow the racing through properly, and although I was only in my twenties, I was a bit old. So I joined Rainbow — basically because I'd run out of money."

As a result, the option of taking up a career in Formula Three had less appeal to Cozy than the opportunity that was presented to him to work with an established act in the form of one Ritchie Blackmore. Maybe Cozy Powell's career would have taken a very different direction if it wasn't for Blackmore encouraging him to come out of musical retirement. As Cozy was quoted in *International Musician and Recording World* in December 1981; "While I was doing the racing I didn't touch a drum kit for about a year and a half, and then quite out of the blue Ritchie Blackmore called up from LA and said he'd seen me playing with Beck at the Roundhouse, and asked me to join Rainbow."

Although Rainbow was a relatively new band when Cozy joined, Blackmore was already a high-profile musician as a result of the work he had done with Deep Purple. As much as Cozy's passion for racing was still there, as a drummer, he had been presented with an offer that was too good to refuse. It may have been the case that beyond money, Rainbow was perhaps an exciting opportunity for Cozy in terms of music. Going into motorsport had been inspired largely by Powell's dissatisfaction at being a session musician and wanting to do something else. Cozy was quoted retrospectively in April 1999 in *Classic Rock*; "I was doing about fifteen sessions a week in London. I had a fixer called Dave Katz who'd ring up and say, 'Do you want to do a film score today, or a pop band, or a folk singer?' It was good for a while, but then it all got a bit jaded because you got the old farts who'd been doing it for years and weren't very good. After a while I'd had enough." It is exciting to think that even though there was probably financial appeal in joining Rainbow, it was also more of an opportunity for Powell to show what he was capable of as a full member of an established band.

Cozy was quoted in *Modern Drummer* in November 1984 on what his time away from music meant to him prior to joining Rainbow. Also, in this interview, he stipulated that is wasn't just about money and that it was necessary that Rainbow was of musical interest to him too; "I had so much enthusiasm when I came back. It was a good offer, musically, although financially it wasn't a great offer. But I've always made my moves for the music, not the finance at all. If you don't enjoy it and you get ten grand a week, the money will go on booze, drugs or whatever else you have to take to make yourself feel better. It's never been the money, although I've been accused of that in the past. But the thing with Rainbow looked so good that it enticed me back into the business after the motor racing. Ritchie's ideas sounded so good and the first album we did (*Rainbow Rising*) was really good, I thought. Ritchie said that when he left Purple it was because rock 'n' roll had become a bit boring. What he wanted to do was put on a really outrageous stage show with a lot of movement and a lot of power, which was right up my street. He spent a lot of money on the set, had big backdrops, a great rainbow that lit up, and it was very exciting. We were putting on a show — an event. It was the forerunner to Kiss and that whole thing."

Cozy was introduced to Blackmore's sense of humour early on in their professional relationship. Bassist Jimmy Bain was quoted in April 2014 in *Classic Rock* as he recalled Cozy's audition for the band. Blackmore had a nonchalant way of auditioning drummers. When Cozy arrived, the joke was on them; "The guy (previous candidates for the position of drummer) would come in, set up his kit, and we'd go to the other side of the building and play pool. When he got comfortable, Ritchie would start this really fast riff: dat-dat-dat-dat-dat-dat... I'd join in on bass, and the drummer would start playing along. That would be great for five minutes. After twenty minutes the guy would be falling apart. Ritchie and me would stop playing and go back to the pool table without saying a word. We did this about fourteen times and nobody even came close. And then Cozy arrived. Ritchie goes into his dat-dat-dat-dat-dat-dat routine. We do this for about forty-five minutes and the tempo doesn't fluctuate. We finish that, and before we could say anything Cozy starts another beat on the double bass drum. We were trying to fuck him up, and he turns it around on us. He was in."

There were ups and downs in the dynamic between Cozy Powell and Ritchie Blackmore. Immense pranks and practical jokes as well as stormy fallings out within the band were a key theme. The live shows with Rainbow were always full of excitement and electricity though. It is with Rainbow that Powell delivered his phenomenal drum solo in accompaniment with Tchaikovsky's '1812 Overture' (it was mentioned in *Sounds* in August 1974 that Powell used to do this as an encore with his band, Hammer). Cozy was quoted retrospectively in April 1999 in *Classic Rock*, regarding his intentions in his performances of such solo; "Basically for ten minutes or so, I try to take people out of their everyday reality. When I'm onstage, I'm an entertainer first and a drummer second."

Powell was quoted in *Beat Instrumental* in January 1976 on what he considered to be the importance of using good showmanship to give the band a competitive edge; "The band's going down surprisingly well for a new outfit. I've been over here quite a few times now with various outfits and this one is going down really well. Every date except one so far has been a sell-out which can't be too bad can it? What we've decided to do is to try to go out there and really put on a show. It's very important these days that the kids get their money's worth. I think that if people are going to have to spend so much to go and see concerts then I'm sure that they'd rather see a show put on than watch a bunch of people who walk on, plug in, play and then walk off again. That's especially important at the moment because the scene over here really isn't very good at all. A lot of bands are having a lot of trouble selling out gigs. Probably the only bands who are really pulling massive crowds at the moment are people like The Who, Zeppelin, The Stones and maybe Jethro Tull. Anybody else who tells you that things are going brilliantly on a massive scale just isn't telling the truth."

When Cozy first joined Rainbow he still had his Ludwig kit but it was when he did his first tour with the band in Japan, Cozy was approached by Yamaha. They wanted him to play their drums. Cozy was quoted in *International Musician and Recording World* in December 1981 regarding his response to Yamaha; "I said alright prove it, build me a better kit and if it's better, I'll use it. And they built me a bigger kit. They sent a guy who sat behind me while I played for two gigs, and he drew the angles, watching my hands, making notes on what I hit the most, and what rim sizes I wanted. I wanted metal rims for the bass drums, something that was unheard of. They had to set up this special machine to make these rims for my drum kit. No other Yamaha kits have got them."

A custom kit indeed! Mr Powell knew what he liked. So much so that when asked about it in the same interview, he stipulated that he wasn't really able to recommend the ideal kit to other drummers on the basis that his was so customised and thus not available for general purchase. In the same article, Cozy was quoted; "But I used, on the last Japanese tour, a kit which they (Yamaha) supplied, straight out of the boxes, straight from the shop. I tuned it up on stage and it sounded fantastic, really good. So I know the drums are alright and they haven't just made me a fantastic super-dooper kit and the rest are all rubbish. I use Yamaha now and they endorse me so obviously I get the kits free; but if they weren't any good, I wouldn't bother, I'd use another kit."

Cozy's approach to drumming seemed to have so many paradoxes; playing with passion and purpose yet not wanting to overdo it in terms of practicing, knowing what he wanted from his kit but not having a particular system for tuning it. He was quoted; "Would you believe I don't tune my drums in any specific way? I can pick a drum kit up and I can tune it the way I hear it. I don't know what it is I hear... when you use big sticks and you hit them hard you can't be that fussy about tuning because the tuning is going to go off. I'll try to get an octave from the top tom to the floor and the notes in between are a third and a fifth, but I don't tune to any specific note. That's the way I tune the toms, and on the snare drum I've got the snares quite slack and they're just on and resting on the skin, then I'll turn it maybe quarter or half a turn. So when I hit it I've got the crack because the top skin is fairly tight and when I hit the drum I use a rim shot virtually every time and I use the sound of the snare drum itself, which is a wood shell Yamaha. You're going to get a different sound whatever drum you're using. If it's a Ludwig metal shell you're going to get more of a ring and trying to get rings out of drums (isn't easy)."

Notably there's a lot of subject specific language in this quote from Cozy but I've included it because if you know a bit about drumming then it's a real eye opener regarding how Cozy got his sound. If some of what Cozy was talking about there goes over anyone's head though, I trust that such content is still reflective of the extent to which he put a lot of thought into what he was doing and how we was going to go about getting his sound.

Powell's rapport with Yamaha lasted him well throughout his drumming career. He was quoted in *Modern Drummer* in November 1984; "I've used a Yamaha kit for six years now. They're very well made and very good drums. It's a bloody good kit. Obviously, I have a lot of spares so the kit always stays in tip-top condition, although I've had the same kit for a long time." The Trigger's broom of drum kits!

Ritchie Blackmore had formed Rainbow on the basis of a number of factors. Although he had been a pioneering member of Deep Purple in 1968 (he named the band after his grandmother's favourite song), the band had reached the point where he was unhappy with the musical direction it was taking. By 1975, the third line-up of Deep Purple had become much more funk and soul orientated as a result of the musical influences of David Coverdale and Glenn Hughes.

During the making of Deep Purple's *Stormbringer* in 1974, Blackmore was starting to lose interest. The album was worlds away from the hard rock that was predominantly a trademark sound for the band and indeed Blackmore. As a result of this, the remaining members of Deep Purple were not at all surprised when the *Stormbringer* album was a key catalyst for Blackmore deciding to leave the band in 1975. David Coverdale was quoted in August 1975 in the *New Musical Express*; "Ritchie was worried about the direction he thought the band might be headed in. He didn't like the soul that was creeping into the band. See, what Ritchie regards as funk are things like 'Sail Away' and 'Mistreated' and that's the direction the rest of us saw the band headed in."

Luckily for Blackmore, he had already worked on some sessions with Ronnie James Dio around the same time. Essentially, this was the basis on which Rainbow was formed and in 1975, the band's first album was released, *Ritchie Blackmore's Rainbow*. The album was recorded at Musicland Studios in Munich, Germany with all members of Dio's band,

Elf, sans their guitarist of course.

Cozy was yet to be in the picture. However, when it came to doing Rainbow's first live tour, Blackmore felt that himself and Dio were the only members of the band who would be capable of cutting it on stage. Therefore, it was time for what would become one of many Blackmore style personnel changes in Rainbow. Whilst Gary Driscoll had played drums on the studio album, Blackmore recruited Cozy having been impressed with his work with Jeff Beck as well as his solo work. Successful audition accounted for, a shared sense of humour and enthusiasm for practical jokes possibly sealed the deal.

Throughout the early years of Rainbow (the band had its first non-stop run between the years of 1975 to 1984 prior to Blackmore actually going back to Deep Purple), it really did seem like there was no going back for Blackmore. Powell was quoted on the matter in *Sounds* in June 1979; "Ritchie just doesn't want to know. He isn't interested. He must have been asked to reform the band at least half-a-dozen times, but the fact is that he considers Deep Purple to have been a good group while it was going, but now that it's finished he'd rather just look back and say, 'Well, we were very successful, we made a lot of records, set a lot of trends and I'd rather leave it at that.' What he's doing now is Rainbow, that's what he believes in, it's what we believe in. If he did reform Deep Purple it would be a mistake, it's much better to have your memories and leave things the way they are. If it did happen it would just be a bunch of musicians getting together again to make bread and Ritchie's not into that, he's already made his money. What he's interested in is getting Rainbow to the top and he'll stop at nothing until the band's there. And I'd go along with that as well."

Famous last words eh? Oh well, I guess a lot can change in a very short space of time in the music business. Besides, it is absolutely plausible that Cozy's understanding of Blackmore's stance on Deep Purple was not misplaced at the time. When Blackmore left Deep Purple in 1975, it really did seem to be the case that he was done with it. Blackmore was quoted in the *New Musical Express* in August 1975. When asked about the fact that he had left Deep Purple three months earlier, Blackmore replied, "Physically that is, spiritually, I left about a year ago." In the same article, Blackmore was quoted; "I made the best of it. I was a bit tired of the ideas and the personnel, it was all a bit routine..."

With the line-up for the tour having been established as Ronnie James Dio on vocals, Jimmy Bain on bass, Tony Carey on keyboards, Cozy Powell on drums and of course Ritchie Blackmore on guitar, the tour commenced on 10th November 1975 in Montreal. A computer controlled rainbow consisting of hundreds of light bulbs was the centrepiece for the live performances.

By the time the second album, *Rainbow Rising*, had been released in 1976, the band had become established as a phenomenal live act both visually and musically as well as in terms of the phenomenal energy and presence they brought with them. It was following a gig at Newcastle City Hall in September 1976 that Blackmore decided to fire Carey. He considered his style of playing to be too complex for the overall sound of the band. But struggling to find a suitable replacement, Carey was quickly reinstated. By such time he was often the victim of a range of practical jokes orchestrated by Ritchie and Cozy.

Cozy was quoted retrospectively in April 2014 in *Classic Rock*, "If Ritchie didn't like someone in the band he would play terrible practical jokes on them. And he hated keyboard players." (I'm not sure that Ritchie Blackmore hated/hates all keyboard players; they have been a significant part of his band line-ups throughout his career. I trust that Cozy's comment here was probably made in a humorous way).

Cozy added, "He was a good keyboard player but he was also a little bit cocky, and if you got like that with Ritchie you were shot down in flames." I'm sure it was nothing massively personal against Carey in particular; Jimmy Bain was also fired from Rainbow too. Cozy was quoted on the matter in *Sounds* in March 1978; "He's a great guy (Jimmy Bain). I really used to enjoy playing with him. But when Ritchie gets an idea in his head, that's how he wants to hear it played. It has to be a certain way with Ritchie, and I guess Jimmy didn't play it exactly the way Ritchie heard it. This is why we've gone through two keyboardists, two bassists, and the rest. So then we had to audition bass players, which is really painful for everybody involved, and now we've got Bob Daisley (ex-Widowmaker), which is working out really well."

Despite the dramas in the band that seemed to range within anything from hilarious to possibly somewhat sadistic, the *Rainbow Rising* album was a success. It is a fascinating example of Cozy's creative and technical ability, particularly within the limitations of the album's recording environment. The album, like the band's debut, was recorded at Musicland Studios. Blackmore was quoted in April 2014 in *Classic Rock*; "We had written 'Stargazer' at rehearsals, and 'Tarot Woman', I believe. The other songs we made up in the studio, as far as I remember. We chose the studios because I'd worked there before. I like to be in Germany when I'm recording."

In the same article, Carey was quoted, "We couldn't get the drums to sound live enough, because it was an archetypal seventies studio with rugs on the wall. So we got a wrecking crew together, hacked up the stairwell and turned it into a concrete tomb. That's how Cozy got his sound."

That's fascinating! That would certainly go a long way towards explaining how the bass drums sound so deep and heavy on the track, 'Stargazer'. Of course, there is a lot to be said for Cozy's drumming technique on that song as well as the recording environment being advantageous. In 1997, Cozy was quoted in *Modern Drummer*; "If you listen to 'Stargazer' from the Rainbow album, there's that sort of "roll" thing. I could do that, on any combination of drums, at the same pace, for quite a long time. It's a statement; you have to play as if you mean it. And that's how I've always approached drumming; playing as if it's my last show ever. I taught myself how to drum and took it upon myself to learn how to project in stadiums. I'd work out a way to hit a drum hard, but not so hard that it would choke. It's the same with a cymbal; you've got to find a balance. If you can hear it in your head and know what you're looking for, then you can build your body up to do what you're hearing."

It sounds like the band had a good laugh in the studio too. In the same feature in *Classic Rock*, resident sound engineer of Musicland Studios at the time, Reinhold Mack was quoted, "I did this only once; Ritchie always asked me about WWII stuff — as if I would know. So me and my assistant rented the gear and stormed into the control room cussing and shouting, almost scaring Ritchie to death. Fairly good acting on my part."

This is awesome. The days of recording the *Rising* album strike me as being just as much about the band having a good laugh as well as technically creating a piece of work that would go on to have a monumental influence in the world of rock and heavy metal. In October 1976, *Melody Maker* reported on the album being honoured with a silver disc. By 1979 it was awarded gold disc status. Additionally, the deluxe edition of the album released in 2011 was awarded gold disc status in 2013; *Rising* by name, *Rising* by nature! It is rare that the *Rising* album doesn't appear in any high-profile top album list of the genre, even to this day.

In May 2016 in *Ultimate Classic Rock*, the article quotes

Cozy from Jerry Bloom's 2006 Blackmore biography *Black Knight* as having said of the album, "I think the idea was to try and capture it as quickly as we could. It wasn't a manufactured record. It was done spontaneously and the musician's input is the way you hear it which is possibly why it's one of the better albums that we did." It comes across that Cozy was a perfect fit for the band at this time, both in what he brought to the table technically as well as his engagement with all of the humour that came with being in Rainbow.

More line-up changes occurred prior to the recording of Rainbow's third album in 1977, *Long Live Rock 'n' Roll*. Cozy seemingly survived all such line-up changes with no problem. I don't feel that it's appropriate to hone in on the gossip angle of things too much because I wasn't there, but there are a range of sources that advocate that whilst most members of Rainbow suffered Blackmore's practical jokes and apparent personal dominance at various points in their stint with his band, Cozy was more than capable of asserting himself. There are quite a few sources out there that advocate that Blackmore probably wouldn't have wasted his time doing practical jokes on Cozy because he didn't feel like dealing with the fallout that could have occurred had Cozy not been happy about it (Colin Hart refers to this in his 2011 book, *A Hart Life*).

Equally, I could go on to give what are ultimately a range of speculative reasons about why various members of Rainbow were fired but essentially, a lot of that is gossip too and in the interests of maintaining authenticity in the telling of Cozy's story, I don't want to do that. The important thing is that in a whirlwind of hirings and firings, Cozy Powell succeeded to be one of the more constant members of Rainbow (for a while anyway!)

In fairness to Ritchie Blackmore, on the subject of the infamous Rainbow hirings and firings, he was quoted in December 1979 in *Sounds;* "If they were good enough, they'd still be in the band. I'm not putting down the other members who were in the band, but no one has ever left Rainbow. It's a fact. Not a confrontation just, well you didn't quite make it, you'll have to do other things. Ronnie is a very good singer — I still like him but he was becoming very lackadaisical. I'm sure if he were here now he would argue the point, but the fact is, Ronnie was not contributing what he should have done, and he knows that. For the last two years I would put down the riff, the progressions, give him the basic melody and he would write the lyrics. I found that in the past year he wasn't really doing that. He was bitching about the fact that it was Ritchie Blackmore's Rainbow. And I'm going, look, I've tried after three years to make it just Rainbow, not my Rainbow. When people leave the band we don't give too many reasons because we don't want to hinder their career. But if someone's not pulling their weight then I will not put up with someone who's second rate. I'm not going to jump onstage and say, 'it's alright ladies and gentlemen, I know they're not very good but they are my friends' like most bands do."

Seemingly, musically, Powell was still meeting Blackmore's high standards. All the album output of this Rainbow era is certainly no less than excellent (your mileage may vary but that's my take on it anyway). Blackmore was quoted in July 1979 in *Sounds*; "Cozy is still with us because you can't get any better than Cozy, you know. He's always up there on stage going crazy, he always pushes me on when I look round. He always gives me that incentive to play because Cozy won't let anybody take it easy."

Also, it is considered by some that in the early days of Rainbow, it was more of a collaborative effort than Ritchie being everyone else's boss. In *Black Knight*, Jerry Bloom quotes Raymond D'addario (Rainbow's production manager) as having said, "Back in the early days it was a band. When Ronnie and Cozy were there they had authority but with the last band it was Ritchie's band and he hired people to be in it basically."

D'addario's perception of the situation is pretty much agreeable. As Cozy himself was quoted in *Sounds* in March 1978; "It's (Rainbow) as democratic as it can be really. Ritchie, Ronnie and myself run the band and amongst the three of us it's democratic. We are credited accordingly. But the bass and keyboard players are on salary. It would be unfair to get somebody in and give them a cut of the action straight away. Besides, there are all sorts of legal entanglements. A band, like it or not, is a corporation these days."

Equally, it seems that Powell may have had an extent of authority (or at least a say in some of the executive decisions) on other elements of the band. With regards to touring, he was quoted in the same *Sounds* feature; "I'm thinking about America a lot now, as that's where we're headed. We've just finished the rest of world tour; Japan, Europe and Britain, you know. We concentrated on the areas that bought the albums first, and now that we've cracked all the other countries, it's time to go Stateside. Most groups do it the other way around, but now we've got gold and platinum albums in those other countries, so it's go west young men. It's difficult for us over there as we are a headlining band, yet we're not. I mean we can headline the Los Angeles', the New York's and Chicagos' but forget about the New Orleans', Miamis' and those places, which are just as important. This is why we have to make such a concentrated effort, but the trouble is that we need to find a band that will have us support them. Most bands don't wanna know. The ideal thing would be to either co-headline or just switch around in the cities in which whomever is the larger draw. It's tricky, musicians' egos and all that. We have to find someone we get on with really well, and we're just gonna hafta work. It's gonna be tough and quite honestly, I don't know if the band will make it over there or not. Like I said, it's a challenge."

It is entirely plausible that in the context of band dynamics, Blackmore and Powell perhaps relied on each other equally. Powell was quoted in *Modern Drummer* in November 1984; "Guitarists are very moody characters. I don't know why I've gotten on with guitarists more than anybody else, but I just seem to have that sympathy with them. I think you have to understand guitarists basically. They're a weird bunch. Nothing like those general sort of statements is there? (laughs)... You've got to be mad to have two pieces of wood and hit things with them. Nobody sane would do that would they? But back to guitar players, I think they want somebody with authority. They need somebody to kick them in the ass all the time. Most drummers who don't get on with guitarists are usually the timid type who aren't going to say their piece. I'm not exactly known for my subtlety. If I don't like something, I say so, but it seems to have done well for me in the past, working with guitar players. They can look back at me and see somebody who is going to drive them through the next part of the show or whatever, and that's basically been what I've been all about."

In June 1983 in *Kerrang!*, Cozy was quoted; "I found I *had* to get involved because they were looking to me to get things together. Ritchie just doesn't want to know. All he wants to do is play his guitar." It very much seems that Cozy was competent in the art of asserting himself amongst some of the strongest of characters. He was quoted in the same edition of *Kerrang!*; "In Rainbow — yeah. There were fisticuffs on a couple of occasions, I remember. But you know, music is music and it gets very personal. I'm not the quietest of people and tend to say my piece which has got me into a lot of trouble in the past."

A respectable point there Cozy. I would guess that it takes a strong extent of passion to be that good at what you do and in Cozy's case, it is plausible that there was a lot of that sort of thing going on. We'll never know for certain but still. In July 1977 in the *New Musical Express*, Cozy's consistent sense of authority and independence came across in how he was quoted; "Ritchie? I don't work *for* him, I work *with* him. The day I work for him, I'll leave. I worked for Jeff Beck for two years and got nowhere. I'm not going through that again."

The element of violence that seemed to come with the territory of being a member of Rainbow is pure comedy. It seemed to go far beyond a good guitar smashing. Cozy was quoted a number of times as having talked so casually about physical fights within the band. What is it with rock stars having fights? Oh well, up to them! (assuming that this stuff wasn't communicated to the media at the time for dramatic effect!)

In June 1979 in *Melody Maker*, Powell was quoted; "I wouldn't say that it's the easiest band in the world to be in; you've got to have a strong arm to last the distance. You need to be good at boxing and every kind of freeform fighting. You have to play to the very best of your ability at all times, or you're liable to get a boot up the arse. It's not for the weak-hearted, that's for sure. I've had thoughts about leaving Rainbow every other month. It's easier to quit, but harder to keep going — and I don't believe in giving up. Ritchie must have been thinking 'I wonder how much longer he's going to take this?' while I was thinking 'how much more can he put up with me?' — it was a battle of wits. This is reflected in the way we play, very aggressive; but in the end we've got great respect for each other. Once we get back together we'll get the new stage show prepared, hopefully new members in and have a few punch-ups. Then everything should be all right!"

It wasn't unusual for people to witness Blackmore's enjoyment of practical jokes, as Peter Makowski recalled in his article in April 2014 in *Classic Rock*, "By the time I

Rainbow

joined the band to cover them for *Sounds* magazine, cracks
were beginning to show. On the flight from Australia to Japan,
Blackmore threw buns at disgruntled First-Class passengers'
heads, and convinced confused staff that he was oblivious to
events." (I'm laughing as I write this to be honest. I know I'm
supposed to remain impartial in the telling of this story but
what a character!)

It was often the case that Cozy was very much involved
with the practical jokes, particularly at The Strawberry Studio,
Château d'Hérouville during the recording of the *Long Live
Rock 'n' Roll* album. The repertoire of practical jokes played
on Tony Carey included, Blackmore jabbing a javelin through
the keyboardist's door while he was still in his room and on
another occasion, Cozy joining Blackmore to brick Carey's
bedroom door up. Again, while he was still in the room.
Bullying or hilarity? I'm not sure. You do the maths. Again
though, in fairness to Ritchie Blackmore, there were times
when Cozy was the instigator of practical jokes; Cozy was
on a ladder outside the window of Blackmore's room and he
used string to manipulate a suit of armour that was in the room
(such is the nature of the weird historical and haunted places
the band liked to stay at for recording). Blackmore wasn't
having it though; he came out of the room and pushed Cozy
off the ladder. It sounds like there was a lot of good banter
when Cozy was in Rainbow, depending on where you sense
of humour sits of course.

It was after the release of *Long Live Rock 'n' Roll* in 1978
and the touring period of it that Blackmore had decided to
take Rainbow in a different direction both commercially
and musically. It was this that would form a key element of
Cozy's decision to leave the band. Jimmy Bain was quoted in
April 2014 in *Classic Rock*; "He (Blackmore) was perturbed
that he wasn't being played on the radio and he decided to
go a different route. He didn't think we were going to get

successful, because *Rising* was too heavy."

In the days of Deep Purple, whether for financial or artistic reasons, Blackmore didn't seem too bothered about radio play. He was quoted in August 1974 in *Guitar* as having said, "(Concerts are) very important, even if it's just to let people know we're still around. We certainly don't get any air play on the radio. People like John Peel won't play us. It's all for housewives. It mustn't be too heavy and too involved. It's got to be short, sweet. It's got to be music you can talk over and have a cup of tea to."

However, by the late 1970s, Blackmore was seemingly more commercially minded. In December 1979 in *Sounds*, it was reported; "This time they're (Rainbow) headlining, partly for added financial reward and partly because they're on their way to their first big A.M. hit in America. I was shown top secret radio figures that showed that 'Since You Been Gone' (from their *Down To Earth* album) has been added to more stations that week than any other record, a fact that the (Polydor) press officer was particularly happy about." It's not that *Long Live Rock 'n' Roll* wasn't well received by fans. It did reasonably well in reviews and the tracks 'Gates Of Babylon' and 'Kill The King' are arguably considered iconic even today.

Whether or not Powell was completely happy with the commercial intentions of the band at the time, he was quoted as advocating for some of the logic behind *Long Live Rock 'n' Roll* in *Sounds* in March 1978; "The last album (*Rainbow Rising*) we did didn't get on the radio much, it was just too heavy. The live album (*On Stage*) didn't get on the radio 'cos it was just too long. But this one is a bit more commercial with a lot shorter tracks and should get some airplay, especially in America."

From the band's perspective though, *Long Live Rock 'n' Roll* had some big shoes to fill as the follow up from *Rainbow*

Rising and commercially, it is understandable as to why any artist would want to aim high in such regard. *Long Live Rock 'n' Roll* was reviewed in April 1978 in *Record World*; "Ritchie Blackmore continues to play a no holds barred style of rock that has made Rainbow a top attraction since the demise of Deep Purple. Singer Ronnie James Dio and Cozy Powell help to spearhead the attack along with Blackmore's swashbuckling guitar style."

In one interview, Cozy alluded to the idea that the song, 'LA Connection' was about Carey leaving the band. If it's true, that's so playground isn't it? Picking on someone and then writing a song about them! Mean but funny, funny but mean! For every instance in which Cozy was unsure about the direction Rainbow was going in, there is no denying that the band and its output was generally well received.

The live album released at the time, *On Stage*, was reviewed with enthusiasm in July 1977 in *Billboard*; "Ritchie Blackmore, guitar powerhouse for Deep Purple, broadcast his musical spectrum when he formed Ritchie Blackmore's Rainbow. Now with the name shortened to Rainbow, this five-man group comes up with a solid effort that should put this band right back into the big leagues. The live double album draws from material on the first two Rainbow LPs as well as containing a thirteen-minute version of Deep Purple's 'Mistreated'. The LP moves from dense rockers to fine electronic blues to a version of 'Greensleeves'. Cozy Powell on drums and vocalist Ronnie James Dio have stand out performances."

By 1979, Blackmore had sacked Ronnie James Dio. Musically, the reason for this was reported as being due to the fact that whilst Dio wanted to continue making the same style of music that had all the features present in the previous three albums, Blackmore was keen to take the band in a direction that had more commercial appeal in terms of getting their music played more on radio and being able to be more successful in the singles charts in both the UK and USA (you can't blame him really, Blackmore was funding Rainbow out of his own money acquired from his Deep Purple days).

Whilst Dio was in the band, there was an emphasis on fantasy-based lyrics featuring tyrants and elaborate mythical stories. Powell was quoted in *Sounds* in June 1979; "We'd just begun rehearsals for the new album and Ronnie was sort of humming and hawing about this and that... his heart didn't seem to be in it, something wasn't quite right. So he'd come to rehearsals and we'd be bashing away at the backing tracks, waiting for him to come up with the vocal lines, and nothing was really happening. So after a couple of weeks of this Ritchie Blackmore said to me, 'What's the deal? Have you noticed anything different?' And I said, 'Well, yeah. He's not exactly one hundred per cent into it, is he?' And this went on and on and I just think Ronnie had either lost interest in the band or interest in singing our particular kind of music. So, like, the writing was on the wall. The thing is, with Rainbow we don't accept anything less than total conviction from the people in the band. Ronnie wasn't giving it as far as we were concerned, so — pfft! It's as simple as that. It wasn't a case of him not singing very well, the guy's a great vocalist and he always will be. It's just that he'd become disenchanted with us and we'd become disenchanted with him and rather than just keep going, plod along like a lot of bands do, we decided that it would be best to take the trouble right out at source. So we asked him if he wanted something else and he said, 'Yeah, okay' and left. He didn't get fired, we asked him to leave. You can read into that what you can like."

Yet another interview where it comes across that Cozy was speaking with candour. His explanation of Dio leaving Rainbow was much more coherent than Ritchie Blackmore's answer to the question in an interview on topical music TV show at the time, *Countdown;* "Well, Ronnie, it was a case of he had so many ideas but they weren't ideas to do with music. They were more about getting married, buying books and painting his toilets and things. It wasn't really what we had in mind for music."

By 1979 when Graham Bonnet was recruited as Rainbow's new vocalist, the *Down To Earth* album (the only one he made with the band before he got fired) included the hit singles 'All Night Long' and the Russ Ballard penned 'Since You Been Gone'. It's funny because many people seem to be of the opinion that from the *Down To Earth* album and thereafter, Rainbow's sound wasn't as heavy as the band's musical output first portrayed. I don't think that's actually the case (listen to 'Death Alley Driver' from the 1982 album, *Straight Between The Eyes* as an example or indeed 'Fire Dance' from the 1983 *Bent Out Of Shape* album).

However, whilst Cozy was capable of playing across a range of genres, at the time he considered that the musical direction that Rainbow was going in wasn't right for him. In May 1982 in *Kerrang!*, it was reported that during the time of the tour for the 1979 *Down To Earth* album, Cozy was certain that Rainbow's musical direction at the time really wasn't something that he wanted to be part of; "Rumors about some of the group were beginning to fly, with Cozy Powell seen signing his autograph "ex-Rainbow". Bonnet too caused some confusion in Japan where the girls like their rock singers to look the part! Bravely he stuck to his guns, or should that be beach shirts?"

"By the end of the summer Cozy's departure was just a poorly kept secret and he played his last Rainbow gig as they headlined the first *Monsters Of Rock* festival on 16th August 1980. His main reason for leaving was the increasing commerciality of Rainbow for which he felt Blackmore had sacrificed too much and his replacement, an American called

Bobby Rondinelli from the outfit by the name of Samantha actually came over for the Donington gig."

It would seem that Powell didn't lack confidence in the musical abilities of Rainbow's line-up for the *Down To Earth* album, it really does come across that his problem was with the musical direction of Rainbow rather than with the abilities of the musicians themselves. Powell was quoted in *Sounds* in June 1979 where he sounded enthusiastic about the line-up; "It's a bit like being a footballer, if you're not doing your job then it's, like, the reserve team or a transfer. That's why the new Rainbow has taken a year to get together, we were waiting to find the right people, people who could consistently give one hundred per cent. And I think it's going to turn out to be pretty good."

Geoff Barton discussed Rainbow's change of direction in his article, "Lost In The Danger Zone — a rambling treatise on the merits (and demerits) of the new Rainbow line-up" in *Sounds* in July 1979 (note that everything in brackets are his words and not mine!); "The old – 'I'm the man on the silver mountain', and the new – 'I lose my mind when we're makin' love'... compare and contrast, add and subtract, weigh and evaluate. In line with Ronnie James Dio's departure and Rainbow's new, much touted "commercial consciousness", this new LP, *Down To Earth* (aptly titled as it turns out), contains no titles like 'Sixteenth Century Greensleeves' and 'Stargazer', no sword and sorcery slanted lyrics, a tight rein being kept on the quality of wild romance. Instead, we have numbers called 'All Night Long', 'No Time To Lose' and 'Love's No Friend', songs that adhere closely to women, getting' down and havin' a real good time (note if you please the all-important use of the apostrophe in the latter half of the preceding sentence). But don't despair AOR haters, contrary to previous reports, Rainbow most definitely haven't "done a Foreigner" and mustered an all-out assault on US drive time radio. No, the music's hard driving and much the same, it's just that Dio's leave taking (did he fall or was he pushed? Will we ever find out?) and Roger Glover's subsequent arrival has made for this natural lyrical progression (to be cruel, it could be labelled "regression"). And being a fan of Kiss, a band that associates itself with some of the dumbest R&R words known to mankind, I shouldn't really be complaining. But somehow it doesn't seem right. While on one hand the band must be commended for keeping matters short and simple on this album (no meandering three and a half hour versions of 'Catch The Rainbow' for instance), I nonetheless feel myself pining for the days of yore, when even the band's more basic tracks such as 'Starstruck' and 'Long Live Rock 'n' Roll' had an epic feel, were much more than mere rollocking good time four minute throwaways. Still, times change and so do bands."

Barton continued, "I agree with Powell's comments a few weeks back, this is the strongest version of the band so far, in the keyboard department in particular, Don Airey, making his predecessors sound like ham-fisted singalong pub piano players. Not so keen on Bonnet's vocals however, whilst he's got a hell of a lot more range and variation to his chords than Dio, to my ears on this album he tries a trifle too hard, his shouts 'n' screams seemingly resulting from a conscious effort on his part. 'All Night Long' is the album opener, one of the unpretentious stompers mentioned earlier. 'Eyes Of The World', an Oldfieldesque intro leading into some hugely entertaining heavy metal dramatics, Powell thundering away like he was Thor."

After offering his personal opinion on each of the album's tracks and comparing them to other songs around at the time, Barton advocates of the controversial 'Since You Been Gone', "I can't understand why they decided to record it when Clout's rendition of the number has been such a big hit so recently. And I can't imagine Blackmore stooping so low as to play this live, let alone smash his Strat at the end of it. It really is the pits."

Barton concludes his review of *Down To Earth*, "This album is definitely worth listening to but in the days of the £5 album, is it truly worth buying? After infinitely careful consideration I can't bring myself to award it any more than three (out of a possible five) stars. That should tell the tale." Bloody hell Barton! Calm down mate! Does he really think that *Down To Earth* is *that* bad? I personally don't but the fact is that many people did and this is evidently reflected in how the album was reviewed and indeed, what it ultimately meant for Cozy's career as in, *Down To Earth* seemed to be the point at which regarding Rainbow, Powell had decided he'd had enough.

It sounds like Cozy was classy about the handing in of his notice; the band's tour manager at the time, Colin Hart, considers so in his 2011 book, *A Hart Life*. Nevertheless, with Cozy Powell and Graham Bonnet both out of Rainbow, they teamed up to work on Bonnet's solo project; his solo album, *Line-Up* was released in 1981 (their most notable single, 'Night Games' was in the UK top ten singles chart) but thereafter, both Bonnet and Powell moved on to other projects.

As ever, Powell was not just the drummer who turned up, played and then forgot about it. It seemed that he took an active interest in how the music was being promoted. In *Kerrang!* in April 1982, Cozy was quoted as he offered his opinion on how the record company had managed the singles from Bonnet's *Line-Up* album; "The track 'SOS' is great but they didn't put it out as a single. They put out 'That's The Way That It Is' — that's a nice song but it's not a single. 'SOS' was written as one. Next thing you know... oh dear... then they released 'Liar', that's a bit old hat for a single. I often wonder who makes the decisions in record companies to put out singles. Maybe they ask the tea lady what she likes." (Graham Bonnet though, what a voice! Four octaves and so much power! His *Line-Up* album is well worth a listen).

Powell was quoted in April 1982 in *Kerrang!*; "I don't mind doing Russ Ballard songs — the reason I didn't want to do 'Since You Been Gone' with Rainbow was because I didn't think it was a Rainbow song. 'All Night Long' was written before I heard 'Since You Been Gone', which was a great single. I like the way it was structured but 'Since You Been Gone' was a bit lightweight. When I joined Rainbow it was a very hard-rocking band. We did *Rainbow Rising*, which I still think is the best album Rainbow's ever done. But then it started to get lighter and lighter. I was asked to do this song by a South African girl group called Clout — 'Since You Been Gone?' and I went 'fucking no way, leave it out, this is a bloody rock band, not a bunch of poofs.' Anyway, we did it and that's another reason I left. Look at the state of the band now. That's being a little unfair but... 'Since You Been Gone' was a bit too commercial and wasn't right for Rainbow, who'd done stuff like 'Stargazer'."

Rainbow's *Down To Earth* album did do well. In terms of the charts (it got to number six in the UK), radio play and reviews. Evidently, the band just wasn't Powell's cup of tea by that point. Fair play for him for (seemingly) prioritising what he believed in musically. In *Billboard* in August 1979, *Down To Earth* was reviewed; "Heavy metal enthusiasts will like this effort as it features Ritchie Blackmore on guitar, Roger Glover on bass and Cozy Powell on drums. All are favourites in this genre. Aided by the vocals of Graham Bonnet and keyboard work of Don Airey, this LP never slows down for a minute on its eight cuts. There are some surprisingly commercial moments, as on 'Since You Been Gone' though other cuts leave room for Blackmore to do his thing on guitar."

In all fairness to Powell, he was consistent in expressing his dislike for 'Since You Been Gone' and he clearly had a voice on the matter whilst still with Rainbow. He was even quoted in the *Down To Earth* tour programme; "Whether we'll be playing it live depends on whether Ritchie and I have an argument. The trouble is though that we only talk after a bout! But seriously, the reason that I'm not too keen on it is that I just don't think that it's heavy enough for Rainbow."

Cozy was quoted retrospectively in April 1999 in *Classic Rock*, "Towards the end of Rainbow, I felt that a couple of singles were selling out. Rainbow was formed to be a hard rock band, but although I liked tracks like 'Since You Been Gone' (a top ten hit for Rainbow in 1980), I didn't think they were right for Rainbow. By then the band had veered off on a tangent, and Ritchie had started playing with his back to the audience — it all started to get a bit thin. A bit like a love affair, we'd grown tired of each other."

Importantly though, I must stipulate here that this is a retrospective quote and in later years, Cozy and Ritchie did patch things up. This is stated in a range of sources, for instance, in June 1983 in *Kerrang!*, Cozy was quoted; "I stayed with Rainbow until Ritchie and I fell out over a number of points, then I thought it best to leave. It was a mutual decision and he and I are still good friends."

Maybe things were just a bit sore at first not long after Powell had left Rainbow. It was in December 1981 that he was quoted in *International Musician and Recording World;* "I left because I thought the band was going no further and Ritchie Blackmore has got an ego bigger than mine, and after five years we couldn't go on any longer, we'd just had enough of each other. The guy's a very good guitarist but familiarity breeds contempt. Also, I didn't like the direction the music was going in — it was too poppy and too away from what we'd done when we first started. Ritchie for some reason wanted to be a pop star and yet he's still trying to kid himself that he's still Ritchie Blackmore, hard and moody. Maybe you can kid the public but you can't kid yourself."

Also, more importantly perhaps, Cozy's work with Rainbow leaves behind a phenomenal legacy of his achievements not only as a drummer, but as an effective contributor to a high-profile band. Cozy has writing credits on a number of the songs on the albums, his solos during the live shows were stratospheric (get hold of some of the bootlegs if you can for further evidence and enjoyment of this, I recommend one called *Roger's Perfect Party*, named as such due to the gig being on Glover's birthday on 30th November... it features a rousing rendition of Cozy's '1812 Overture' solo). Ultimately, Powell was with Rainbow for a solid five years before deciding to move onto pastures new.

Chapter Six:
Michael Schenker Group (1980–1982)

In September 1980, *Record Mirror*, announced Cozy's new role; "Cozy Powell has been confirmed as the drummer for the Michael Schenker Band (sic) for their forthcoming tour, ending weeks of speculation. But Powell, who made a "planned" departure from Rainbow after the Castle Donington Festival last month, hasn't yet said whether he'll stay with Schenker after the tour."

It is understandable as to why Powell may have wanted to keep his options open. By this point in his career he had proven himself to be versatile and of value to so many bands, I can see the logic in him not wanting to be tied down; very plausible logic in view of Michael Schenker's reputation perhaps!

The important thing to remember about Cozy's time in this group is that he was working with Michael Schenker; that is to say that dramas, turbulence and in-band fighting probably came with the territory for anyone who worked with the German guitarist. To shed some background on this, prior to Cozy having any professional involvement with Schenker, it was already the case that the latter had a reputation for sometimes being quite a volatile character to work with.

Michael Schenker's career began as an early member of Scorpions. The band was founded by his brother, Rudolph. After a stint playing lead guitar with the band UFO in the mid-seventies (and then again at various later points), Schenker formed his own band in 1978. Schenker's debut in the Scorpions was when he was just sixteen years old. He had the talent and the music business had been a part of his life from an early age. Whilst Schenker was in UFO and prior to forming his own band, it wasn't uncommon for shows to be cancelled mid set as a result of him storming off stage due to a mood swing about something or other. Immaturity or just personality? Who knows!

By the time Cozy came to work with Schenker, the guitarist already had a reputation for being difficult to work with. This wasn't Cozy's first time working with a larger than life moody character in his career but equally, there are a number of instances in which Cozy was quoted in a way that makes it seem like artistically and musically, he and Schenker just didn't click. They didn't seem to have that rapport that was apparent between Cozy and Blackmore in Rainbow.

On his differences with Michael Schenker, Cozy was quoted in *Metal Hammer* in February 1988; "I was fired from that band, and it was a great shame. And I still don't know why to this day — I think it was a clash of personalities. I told Michael I didn't want to rehearse for eight hours a day, seven days a week. But because he's German, he likes to do that sort of thing. I don't."

In the same interview, Cozy explained how whilst with the Michael Schenker Group, he played on two of the tracks on Robert Plant's first solo album, *Pictures At Eleven*. Plant wanted Powell to play on more of the album (Phil Collins finished the rest of the album and Barriemore Barlow did the first tour) but Powell, ever the professional, was already contractually committed to Michael Schenker and endeavoured to honour that; "I was already contracted to tour with Schenker. I had to leave the recording of *Pictures At Eleven* to tour with the Michael Schenker Group. So I only did the two tracks. But I would definitely have done the rest of the album and I would have toured had I been asked. But I'm not the complete cunt some people think I am so I did honour the contract. Michael was paying my wages so I stayed with him. In retrospect I probably should have gone with Robert."

Cozy was later quoted on the matter in *Modern Drummer* in 1997; "I did the whole album and Phil (Collins) came in and finished it. It's not a bad thing to have Phil Collins as a "deputy". I had to go on tour with the Michael Schenker Group and couldn't complete the album. Robert told me that Phil came in, heard my tracks, and said, 'There's nothing wrong with these. I couldn't do any better' — That's a real compliment."

As with the turbulence of many bands, the Michael Schenker Group had numerous personnel changes that coincided with the time that Cozy was involved with the band. In 1982, vocalist Gary Barden was fired in favour of Graham Bonnet. Powell was instrumental in Bonnet's recruitment to the band. As Powell was quoted in *Kerrang!* in April 1982; "Believe it or not it wasn't my idea. I didn't suggest Graham because I thought people would draw too many conclusions. We had a few singers on the shortlist before Graham was ever discussed. In the end Michael said he was writing songs with someone like Graham in mind. So I said 'If you're writing with his voice in mind let's get him over. There's no harm in trying it', I didn't know if he was going to carry on with his solo career or not but he came over and is still with us, so hopefully it'll work out okay."

In the same interview, Cozy seemed keen to stipulate that Graham Bonnet joining the Michael Schenker Group would not result in the band sounding like Rainbow; "Michael's written the bulk of the material as he has done most of the time. There's been a lot written about Graham not being able to write lyrics and melodies. That's not strictly true. In fact he wrote most of 'All Night Long'. What's happening is that we're all working together and if the lyrics don't work out, then we'll get a lyricist in. Or somebody we know within our sphere of writing friends to help us out. It's not the end of the world, anyone who can write lyrics like... well 'All Night Long' aren't exactly the most inspired lyrics you're ever gonna hear. 'Her brain's all right but her...' I can't even remember it was so naff. But that was a hit, so I think the lyrics we've got so far don't sound too bad. If we can't come up with as good a set of lyrics as Roger Glover did with Rainbow it's a poor show." (I don't think Powell was being disparaging of Roger Glover or Glover's song writing abilities here. It's just that Cozy really wasn't happy with the direction that Rainbow was taking around that time).

Cozy elaborated in the same interview upon being asked by the interviewer, "Surely the music business has changed in the past five years or so and you can't just do two songs on a side like Rainbow did on *Rising*?" (that's a bit of an exaggeration from the interviewer there, the songs on *Rainbow Rising* weren't that long, but still...).

Cozy's response was; "That's right. Obviously we are gonna change. I just change a lot slower than everybody else. I'm old fashioned if you like. I'm not saying a band should do an album of fifteen-minute tracks per side. It was just the whole idea of Rainbow when I joined was not to be a pop band. If I'd wanted to join a pop band I could have joined Suzi Quatro or something like that. Michael Schenker Group is a hard rocking or heavy metal band — I don't know what you want to call it. The way I see my role in Michael Schenker Group is to harden it up and not let it get too soft. That's just my personal opinion."

Even whilst he was with Michael Schenker Group, Cozy was honest about his feelings and expectations of what sort of mileage he perhaps had with the band. He was quoted in *Kerrang!* in April 1982; "I was getting disenchanted around Christmas time. I was working with Robert Plant and I thought, 'is it worth carrying on?' Then Michael and I had a couple of barneys (sic) after Gary and Paul left, Michael said we had to pull together if we were going to make it. So I thought 'alright, let's give the band a bit of time, let me drop all my solo projects and I'll concentrate solely on Michael Schenker Group. If it works out, great. If it doesn't, at least I've given it my best shot', that's what I'm doing now, I've knocked everything else on the head and so the band is a three-piece unit backing Graham. It's either going to work or it isn't. We've written seventeen tracks for the new album of which we'll pick the best. Michael's obviously come up with the basic ideas and Chris and I have done our bit. Being a drummer I don't contribute much to the writing. I just add more to the arranging than the writing. But I've come up with a few bits and pieces here and there. Graham has now got to go and put his lyrics and melodies on. Then we'll get together in a week or ten days and get on with it. I'm sick and tired of sitting on my arse."

At the time of the interview, Powell was looking forward to getting to work in the studio with the Michael Schenker Group, when asked about when they would start recording, Cozy was quoted; "In about three weeks. We're doing it in the Chateau in France where I did *Long Live Rock 'n' Roll* with Rainbow. So that'll be good because we liked the drum sound there. If we start in the middle of April, it should be out in the summer. There are no plans for live gigs at the moment but I imagine September, either here or Japan. We'll concentrate on the two markets that have helped us."

I would imagine that Cozy's experience at the Chateau in France with Michael Schenker would have been very different to that which he experienced there with Rainbow. The cover notes of the *Long Live Rock 'n' Roll* album refer to the difficulties that the band had in the studio due to what they describe as their paranormal experiences there. The rapport that Powell had with Blackmore was such that he quite possibly had a lot more fun in Rainbow than he did with the Michael Schenker Group. Oh well, at least Powell wasn't too afraid to go back to the Chateau, many perhaps would have been!

The strictly professional dynamic between Powell and Schenker, i.e., one with perhaps minimal personal rapport was implied when in April 1982 in *Kerrang!*, Cozy was quoted on how he had to constantly address the rumours that Schenker had heard about the possibility of Cozy joining another band; "There was a time, towards the end of last year, when I was working with Robert Plant when everybody was asking 'Is he joining Led Zep, The Who, Status Quo?' All these bands you sort of dream about. I haven't heard from any of them. Maybe there were a lot of drummers' vacancies last year and my name, because I was supposedly dissatisfied with Michael Schenker Group, was linked. That's nice and it doesn't hurt to have your name in the papers every week. At the same time it was a bit disconcerting for Michael, 'cos every week he'd ring up and go 'are you joining Status Quo?' and I'd have to tell him 'not as far as I know' and the next week it would be 'what is this I see about The Who?' Also working with Robert, people naturally put two and two together and came up with Zeppelin. I don't know what the situation with Zeppelin is, I don't even know if they do."

It must have been frustrating for Cozy having to keep explaining himself to Schenker. Cozy's comments here make Schenker come across as having been paranoid and controlling. I'm completely guessing here but either way, it doesn't sound like they had a very healthy or indeed trusting working relationship. It matters however to point out that as honest as Cozy's comments were in this article, his sense of professionalism (in terms of sticking to what he said he was going to do) is ever present. Cozy continued; "Initially I was going to do the whole album (with Robert Plant) and then it became impossible to do that and Michael Schenker Group. I had to make a choice, and since Michael Schenker Group are paying my wages it would be unfair to go 'shove it lads, I'm going to work on this solo thing so I can make some money'. Although people seem to have given me a terrible reputation of being mercenary and only doing things for money, I actually turned all that down and said to Robert I'd do a couple of tracks and spend the rest of my time working with Michael Schenker. So I ended up doing two tracks... it bothered me when I saw a couple of letters from kids in the music papers. Whether it was sent by kids or journalists trying to stir the shit, we'll never know. But there were a couple of really nasty things that were totally untrue... I mean, I've been ripped off a bit in my career, a lot more than kids will ever dream about. They got the idea that I was just in it for the money because that was a quote that I made jokingly once that I regret now. I just said it for a laugh and it was taken seriously. Everybody's in this business to make money, let's not kid ourselves, but at the same time I could have joined a lot of other bands — not necessarily the ones I talked about a minute ago. A lot of other bands offered me a lot more money than Michael Schenker Group paid me. And if I was in it for the money I would have joined them but I didn't and I've stuck it out with Michael Schenker Group 'cos I believe in the band."

In December 1980, *Record Mirror* commented on Cozy's music from that year; "Cozy Powell kept well to the forefront in 1980; first leaving his old mate Ritchie Blackmore in Rainbow (who may still be in the process of splitting up altogether), then joining the Michael Schenker Group to carry on the metal mayhem. And wasn't it Cozy too, who was hotly tipped as the replacement for John Bonham in Led Zeppelin?"

As with all other projects in Cozy's career, musically

he gave it his all. As unhappy as he seemed about his time in the Michael Schenker Group, his passion for the music in and of itself didn't come across as absent. Cozy was quoted in *Kerrang!* in April 1982; "The material on the last Michael Schenker Group album was a lot better than people made out, but the production didn't bring out the best of the material. The best track probably turned out to be Paul's 'Never Trust A Stranger'. It's more of an LA sort of thing and Nevison did a very good job on that. But the harder tracks had a lot more balls. 'Mad Axeman', 'Let Sleeping Dogs Lie' (Cozy shares writing credits on this track) sounded a bit too clean for my liking, it wasn't really nasty enough. So the material on the new album will be a lot nastier. Michael Schenker Group go Motörhead or whatever!... there's no plans to get another keyboard player. I don't think we need a keyboard player; we can get away with Michael and Chris using Moog pedals to give us all the colours we need. This band is a lot stronger and harder. Keyboards tend to knock the edge off and smooth it out. I want to go the other way and get it a bit nastier than it's been. So at the moment, unless we really need one, we won't... and no, it won't be Don Airey. I mean we might as well get Ritchie on second guitar if that was to happen!"

On what was perhaps a less diplomatic day for Powell though, he came across as really cheesed off about the production of the Schenker album that he played on. In December 1981, Cozy was quoted in *International Musician and Recording World*; "With Michael I'd always admired his playing from a distance. I'd never really taken much notice of him, I knew he was very good and suddenly an opportunity came up to play with him, which I did, and I was extremely impressed with his playing. I liked his material although I thought his first album was possibly a little bit lightweight. I heard the material for the second album, which I thought was terrific, but unfortunately the producer, Ron Nevison, heard it a different way and wanted to make it sound American. There was so much power on the tape but he didn't get it across on the disc. It's bloody awful production but I wasn't there when he did it. That's Ron Nevison for you."

In the same interview, Powell elaborated on his frustrations; "On the *MSG* album it took a week of me bashing away in Air Studios for hours and hours on end so this bloody primadonna could get the sound he thought was right. In the end he ended up nearly erasing a bass drum track because he didn't hear it. A week! Do me a favour, it doesn't take that long to get it. If you're going for a live drum sound, as long as the room's right and the drummer knows what he's doing it doesn't take more than about ten minutes to get the sound. As long as the drums are tuned and ready to go it's down to mic placing. You just put two ambient mics say, ten feet away from the drums either side in stereo, mic them up all close and leave the desk flat."

Cozy's comments here really reflect the extent to which he engaged with the production process in his work as in, even if production wasn't his role on any given project, he had an extent of ability in that area that really brought something to all of the bands he worked with, as would prove to be the case in his work with Black Sabbath.

Additionally, Cozy's passion for drumming (and indeed, delivering on good showmanship) didn't seem to be marred by the personnel frustrations he probably experienced with Schenker. In June 1983 in *Kerrang!*, Powell was quoted; "I used some pyrotechnics on the last Schenker tour and that was the first time I'd used so much gunpowder — it nearly burnt me every night. All I'm trying to do is frighten the audience! And attempt to blow up the stage. I will, eventually, blow the stage up. Although the flames look pretty devastating, it's fairly safe. It's all in a metal box and kept under control. The flame jets go up to ten feet in the air and we have three of them. I did have four, but got a bit burnt. The audience not only sees the effect, it feels the heat (dangerous if you wear contact lenses, incidentally). And if you think it's hot out front, imagine what it's like on the drum kit."

When giving his reasons for leaving the Michael Schenker Group, Cozy was quoted in *Kerrang!* in June 1983; "When I joined Michael, he asked me what I thought about things then put me in charge ('You sort it out') Fine. Up until the point where we disagree. Then I'd tell him, 'Alright, you run the band. It's your band anyway', in the end it got to the point where we couldn't play together any longer. The amount of rehearsing finally did me in. We spent three months rehearsing — every day. Now to me rehearsals are a very important part of the show, but you don't spend three months in a rehearsal studio. My job is to play onstage, and that's where I play best. If it's all too perfect, it becomes sterile. Anyway, it wasn't a jazz-rock group but an out-and-out heavy metal band. You don't *rehearse* heavy metal, it's very much off the cuff. That's the basic reason I left Michael. You see he's a bit slow and has to work out every note and go over it time and time again. I said: 'Look, I can't stand all this rehearsing any longer. It's just getting stupid', I could have taken the money and shut up, but that's not my way. Off I went. You have to learn to live with it. I've been in so many controversial bands, particularly Rainbow and Michael Schenker Group."

In the same article, Cozy was quoted; "It started off good (with Michael Schenker), then dwindled away. I thought it was all a bit sad actually. I knew it was coming. I left — or rather was asked to leave. And then Graham Bonnet left rather quickly, it was all in the winds. But of course you can't say too much. It's all behind the scenes stuff. You don't want to air dirty washing in public."

There is much class, discretion and gentlemanliness about Cozy here; at the time, rumours circulated that Graham Bonnet had dropped his trousers on stage in a drunken state, causing him to be sacked by Schenker. It wasn't until much later on that Bonnet clarified what had happened. In a candid interview with *Classic Rock* in May 2018, Bonnet was quoted; "It was a time I don't remember too well, I was drinking heavily. A lot of the time I was semi-conscious. I thought that drinking made it better. That was my downfall. We'd all been drinking that afternoon, by show time I was obliterated. I swore at the audience for fucking up my lyrics, they shouted back: 'You cunt!' And then the fly on my jeans split, my dick fell out, and of course the dick became part of the act. I said: 'Here it is, wibble-wobble, see ya!' And I walked off."

Bonnet retreated to his hotel after that. The next morning he made his way back to London to be told by his manager that he'd been fired by Michael Schenker. The very fact that Cozy declined to comment on this when he was interviewed by *Kerrang!* in June 1983 speaks volumes about his generosity and professionalism; he could have indulged the gossip but actively chose not to. Importantly, at the end of his May 2018 interview with *Classic Rock*, Bonnet was quoted; "I have now been sober fifteen years, thank God I'm not that guy anymore."

Besides, if Michael Schenker wasn't happy with Cozy Powell, Stewart Copeland certainly had no complaints when he went to see his fellow drummer play a gig with the Michael Schenker Group (kind of!).

When Copeland wrote gig reviews in October 1980 in *Record Mirror*, he explained of the Michael Schenker Group gig at the Hammersmith Odeon; "As soon as the music died down I whispered the code words. I was hustled down a side corridor so that the panting band could flash past back to their dressing room. I caught a glimpse of Cozy Powell and some sweaty, glittering t-shirts and they were gone. Shit! I had missed the gig. I'd been looking forward to seeing Cozy, who I had last seen drumming with his own group, Cozy Powell's Hammer, before I ever joined a group. He always had a thumpy kind of charm and maybe tonight he would have some licks for me to steal."

In the same piece, Copeland mentions how Lemmy from Motörhead was also there and spoke highly of Cozy's drumming (Cozy and Lemmy worked together on The Young And Moody band's 1981 single, 'Don't Do That' which also featured The Nolans. It charted at number sixty-three in the UK).

The admiration was mutual. In *Rhythm* in October 1987, Powell was quoted on his appreciation of Copeland's drumming; "Stewart Copeland, for example, really drove The Police, but he has his very own individual style which when he got together with Sting and Summers must have really impressed them. I've always done it by being a powerful player, who maybe hasn't got a lot of technique but what technique I have picked up by watching and listening to other people, works fine for me."

Maybe Powell's expectations weren't too realistic when he decided to work with Michael Schenker. Powell was quoted speaking in hindsight on the matter in an interview in *Modern Drummer* in November 1984; "I wanted to join Schenker because again, I thought it would be Blackmore part II, but Schenker was younger and I thought he wouldn't have quite the ego that Ritchie had and was still in the right frame of mind at that time. But Michael Schenker has been known to go up and down in his moods. At the moment, I hear that he's playing better than ever and has really straightened himself out. Michael is his own worst enemy though and has gone through serious phases in the last few years. When I left him, it was because he was not in control of his band anymore. I was more or less running the band. I didn't mind doing it but in the end, even I didn't know what I was doing. It was just a joke. I stayed with Schenker for two years until I just couldn't take it anymore. My leaving received a fair amount of criticism. You probably don't hear about all this in America because the English scene is really completely different but over here (UK) it was big news — front page stuff. Funny, all the bands I've been in during the last ten years haven't really meant anything in America."

In terms of getting on with colleagues and peers in the music industry, you win some you lose some I guess. It seems that Powell ultimately regretted sticking with Michael Schenker, particularly considering that the door of opportunity was wide open for him to be able to work with people who he clicked with better both musically and personally.

Cozy was quoted retrospectively in *Classic Rock* in April 1999; "Planty and I got together, but I'd already agreed to do a tour with Michael Schenker and there was a lot of politics going on. So Phil Collins came into finish the album, which I later regretted. With Michael, the touring schedule was horrendous and it started getting silly."

In the same article, Michael Schenker was quoted; "I didn't have any relationship with him, it was about music, Cozy was a powerful drummer. Technically he wasn't my favourite. Simon Phillips was much more fluid. Cozy was always the favourite of my brother (Rudolf, of the Scorpions). He (Cozy) appeared to me as an individual, he did what he wanted. He came across as a strong personality — he needed to have a function in the band of being more than just a drummer."

Neil Murray's thoughts on the matter were also quoted; "He (Cozy) would always stand up for what he thought he deserved. Cozy didn't like being treated like any old employee. If he was in a band with someone he expected to be virtually as important as the lead singer, the guitarist or whoever was running things."

Fair enough. As in, if more drummers were as passionate and pioneering about the importance of the role of the drummer as Cozy seemed to be, who knows what this could have done for the esteem with which drumming could be held in today.

Cozy Powell's Hammer around 1974. Back row: Bernie Marsden, Frank Aiello and Don Airey. Cozy at the front with Clive Chaman.

At a race meeting in Zandvoort, Netherlands in 1974 indulging in his love for motoring. It was around this time that Cozy had temporarily taken a back seat from music but was enticed back by Ritchie Blackmore when he joined Rainbow the following year.
(Photo Gijsbert Hanekroot / Alamy Stock Photo)

With Ritchie Blackmore during Rainbow's first tour at the
Community Theatre, Berkeley, California, 28th November 1975.
(John Oster)

On the first European tour with Rainbow in 1976 in Liverpool with bassist Jimmy Bain.
(Alan Perry Concert Photography)

A bit of typical irreverence on tour with Rainbow in 1979.
(Colin Hart)

At Newcastle on Rainbow's Down To Earth Tour — his last
with the band. Including a rare moment during the show that
gave Cozy time to catch his breath.

(Alan Perry Concert Photography)

Moving from working with one difficult guitarist to another. With the Michael Schenker Group in 1980.

With Whitesnake in 1982.
Left to right: Colin Hodgkinson, Mel Galley, Cozy, Jon Lord, David Coverdale & Micky Moody.

A serious look for a more serious music with Keith Emerson and Greg Lake, that produced one album and one American tour.

With Forcefield in 1987. A project that Cozy did four albums with. Left to right: Ray Fenwick, Chris Cozens, Cozy, Pete Prescott & Neil Murray.

Promo photo with Black Sabbath at the time they produced the *Headless Cross* album. Left to right: Tony Martin, Tony Iommi, Cozy and Neil Murray.

Throughout his career, Cozy worked with numerous top guitarists. Towards the end he spent time with Fleetwod Mac's creator Peter Green in the Splinter Group as well as encouraging Brian May to step out of the shadow of Queen.

Peter Green's Splinter Group
L-R: Peter Green, Cozy, Nigel Watson, Neil Murray & Spike Edney.

Chapter Seven:
Whitesnake (1982–1985)

Perhaps joining Whitesnake was interesting for Powell on the basis that the band's leader was a vocalist rather than a guitarist. After working with so many bands led by guitarists, Cozy was quoted on the matter in *Modern Drummer* in November 1984; "I don't have to play as loudly, which is nice. I don't have to battle against who knows how many watts of guitar scream. I've always played with guitar players who have seemed to get louder and louder by the week. Ritchie wasn't actually the quietest bloke I'd ever met. Schenker was equally loud. I would think 'could you turn it down?' I hit the drums very hard, but I was still battling against the PA or whatever and it drove me mad. With a vocalist leading the band, the band volume, although it's still loud, has dropped fractionally, which gives me a chance. I say that in one breath, but in the next breath, I must say the pace of our show is very hard. It is frantic."

By the time Cozy was with Whitesnake, he was in his mid-thirties. For all of the experience he'd had in the industry by then and for all of the times he had considered calling it a day to do racing instead, he continued to value the importance of keeping fit for the purpose of drumming well. When asked by *Modern Drummer* in November 1984 about how he kept up with the demands of playing high paced frantic shows, Cozy was quoted as advocating for staying healthy and working ergonomically; "It's not easy to do. Obviously if your show consists of mostly fast and furious numbers, you've got to try to figure out how you're going to get through it. It's a question of pacing the show. Usually the first two or three numbers are just heads down, bang go-for-it sort of things. I've got to get through the first two or three numbers without much of a break, so I'm talking about ten to twelve minutes of non-stop blast, flat out playing. That is draining before the show even starts. When we play America, we'll be supporting and not headlining so it won't be that bad. I try to keep fit. I gave up smoking a couple of years ago, no big deal. I went through a phase of rather heavy drinking and I've cut down on that. If you're going to keep going, you have to take care of yourself. I'm thirty-six, so not exactly a young kid anymore but I'm still competing with kids half my age. They have the energy naturally that I have to work at. When they say the older you get, the more experienced you are, it's true because you have to pace yourself. It takes a hell of a lot more determination to do at thirty-six what you could do at eighteen, playing-wise. I do a lot of outdoor stuff to keep in shape. We have a few army units and I'll go down for weekend courses every couple of months to try and keep myself fit. They're special training courses for people in the service. I know a lot of the people because they used to do security at our concerts. They take me down to their headquarters and we do fitness things. We live outdoors in a tent for a week and that's it. It toughens us up. I do a lot of walking — ten to twenty miles a day with a pack on — and it really does get me tough. It just gives me a little more of a chance to take on an American tour. It's a bit like being an athlete. Some drummers have defied the laws, but they're no longer with us. John "Bonzo", a dear friend of mine, is unfortunately no longer with us. John was a big guy anyway, very strong, but it took him and it took Keith Moon. You can't keep that up. If you're going to start messing about with your body, it's going to give up on you. I like to think that

I can still do what I did ten to fifteen years ago with relative ease because I try to take care of myself."

Working with ex-Deep Purple members was a common theme throughout Cozy's career. First he'd been in Rainbow with Ritchie Blackmore (and later, also Roger Glover) and not long after, it was time for a stint with David Coverdale (and Jon Lord) in Whitesnake. Powell also made an appearance on Jon Lord's 1982 album, *Before I Forget*). Moreover, it was Ian Paice (there's that Deep Purple connection again!) who Cozy replaced when he joined Whitesnake. Notably, if it wasn't for Deep Purple, many high-profile rock musicians around this time would have probably sounded very different. What a band!

On getting the job with Whitesnake, Powell was quoted in October 1987 in *Rhythm*; "David Coverdale said I got the job in Whitesnake because I kicked him up the arse harder than anyone else could and I drove the band along. Now that's a nice thing to do. If you're a drummer you have to drive the band. That's three quarters of it, certainly in heavy rock. It may not necessarily be the case in electronic music, but if you can drive the band along and really punch it, but also do it with some clever technique then that's all the job."

By the time Cozy opted to join Whitesnake, he was very much in demand. He was quoted retrospectively in April 1999 in *Classic Rock*; "David Coverdale kept phoning me up. At the same time, Tony (Iommi) wanted me to join Black Sabbath. In the end I went with Coverdale and had a couple of successful years with Whitesnake. I did all the groundwork for the phenomenally successful *1987* album, and David and I had done a business deal for the arrangements of the album, but when it came to the crunch, the lawyers and businessmen got involved and said, 'The deal has been changed — take it or leave it.' I'm a man of principle, so I walked, and of course the album went on to sell fourteen million units! Aynsley

(Dunbar - the drummer on the *1987* album) came in and virtually copied what I'd done!"

What Cozy said here is entirely plausible; on the track, 'Still Of The Night', there is a lot of that Powell style, heavy bass drum stuff going on. Cozy didn't seem to think well of his last gig (*Rock In Rio* in Brazil in 1985) with Whitesnake either. In the same article, he was quoted retrospectively; "God, it was pathetic! John Sykes wasn't speaking to David, or Dolly, as we called him! There were all these terrible ego trips going down."

It comes across that Cozy's days in Whitesnake were often problematic and uncomfortable. It might not just have been a Whitesnake thing though, Cozy was quoted in *Modern Drummer* in 1997 as he explained the process behind what could often happen to drummers in the industry; "I did all the groundwork for a lot of the hits that came out in the seventies. Some of the time, they would keep the drums. Depending whether I was available for the final tracks, they would use me or somebody else. In those days it was a cut-throat business and you got used to doing pre-production. Sometimes it seems that my whole career has been spent doing pre-production. I did a number of albums for other groups, where I did all the groundwork. It's one of those political things, part of the business, and I really shouldn't complain because I've been on a lot of records that have been hits."

Time to rewind though; when Cozy joined Whitesnake, it seems that he was walking into a lion's den and certainly not one of his own creation.

Whilst Ian Paice was still drumming for Whitesnake, the band had just finished their *Come An' Get It* tour and thus, the recording for the next album, *Saints & Sinners*, began in 1981. All was not well in the band. Guitarist and backing vocalist at the time, Micky Moody was quoted in issue 34 of *Hard Roxx* in 1997; "By '81 people were becoming tired. We had too many late nights, too much partying. We weren't making nowhere near the kind of money we should have been making. Whitesnake always seemed to be in debt, and I thought 'what is this? we're playing in some of the biggest places and we're still being told we're in debt, where is all the money going?' We hadn't got much money out of it and to be told you're 200,000 pounds in debt, when you just had six golden albums. It wasn't just me, 'cos everybody was getting tired, pissed off and losing their sense of identity. It was over by then; we couldn't get any further. It's difficult for a band to go more than three or four years without getting tired of each other and losing ideas. Nothing lasts forever. Everybody wanted to do something different after a few years, a solo album or write with someone else."

It was such disillusions and problems with morale that resulted in Whitesnake's line-up being unstable by December 1981. It wasn't long after that David Coverdale called a band meeting. It was decided that the band would be put on hold for a while and would dissociate from their manager, John Coletta, who had also co-managed Deep Purple between 1968 and 1976. Eventually the turbulence within Whitesnake (it was perhaps dramatised and/or exacerbated by the press in all fairness) was such that by some point in 1982, David Coverdale only had Jon Lord to rely upon as a committed member of the band.

Finally, after much speculation, the new line-up was announced in the UK music press on 13th November 1982. There was much enthusiasm about Cozy being part of the new band line-up.

Slide It In was Whitesnake's sixth studio album. It was released in 1984 and was the band's first album on Geffen Records in America. It was remixed for the release there and as result there are two slightly different versions of the album. It was the band's forth top ten album in the UK; it peaked at number nine. The album re-entered the charts in America in 1988 based on the success of Whitesnake's eponymous album released in 1987.

It was the success of Whitesnake's 1987 album that pushed the sales of *Slide It In* from gold to double platinum status. The recording of *Slide It In* started in 1983 at Musicland Studios in Munich, Germany. The album was produced by Eddie Kramer. Kramer had been recommended to Coverdale by Geffen Records. Evidently, there was a lot of change in the band at the time from many directions. This was seemingly to the detriment of guitarist Micky Moody's morale and indeed, enthusiasm about the album. He was quoted in issue 34 of *Hard Roxx* in 1997; "I realised that as soon as we started rehearsing and playing that it wasn't the same band, it never felt right. Mel Galley is very talented, a good singer, a great guitar player, but that band just didn't work out. Cozy was a great drummer, I always had a lot of respect for him, but he just didn't have any feel for the old Whitesnake sound. Cozy Powell brought with him a bass player called Colin Hodgkinson. Me and David knew Colin in the North East back in the sixties. He was a great legendary bass player, worked with the jazz/blues styles, but he never struck me as the bass player for Whitesnake. It was more the heavy metal attitude, probably because of Cozy's influence. He was a heavier drummer than Ian Paice. There were flames and explosions going on, not really my cup of tea. It seems to me now that maybe Cozy wanted the band to be much heavier and flasher."

Fairly enough, it doesn't seem that Moody was complaining about other musicians on a personal level but simply an artistic one. It is very plausible that Cozy brought a heavy style of drumming to the table when he joined Whitesnake. He and Ian Paice are both phenomenal drummers both technically and creatively but evidently, their sounds are very different; Cozy's was a much deeper and heavier sound due to the large sticks he used and the emphasis he often placed on bass drums. Heavy doesn't mean worse of course; Cozy's heavy drumming did a lot for Rainbow (particularly on tracks like 'Stargazer' and 'Lost In Hollywood'), it's just that Moody was missing the older sound of Whitesnake I suppose. It happens.

In *Modern Drummer* in November 1984, Cozy was quoted on the way he embraced an extent of simplicity for playing in Whitesnake; "Since 1967, I've always used two bass drums on stage and in most of the recordings I've done. This last album, Whitesnake's *Slide It In,* is the first album I've done with a single bass drum. The tracks didn't require (two bass drums). It was just very simple. The drumming on the new album is nothing spectacular. There are some nice little fills here and there, but I was doing a job and the job didn't require two bass drums. The stuff I've been doing lately requires me to keep a very simple rhythm and nothing more. And I'm quite happy to do that, I get my chance in the solo. The stuff I'm doing is very simple though. It makes me laugh a little bit when I see drummers going on with a long explanation about how they worked out this triple handed paradiddle. What's the point? Who in the audience is going to know what one of these things is anyway? I don't know and I'm a drummer. If you said, 'play a ratamaque', I wouldn't even know where to start. It's all rubbish to me. I just play the drums. I don't bother to get into theory. That might piss some people off who read this, but that's how I feel."

In the same feature, Cozy philosophised about the feel of Whitesnake's music and why he felt that it didn't demand the heaviness of drumming that he had used previously when with other bands; "It's basically just that, feel. The tracks are played in a certain way and there's no point in my thundering away. It would spoil the song. The song is the most important part of anything you do. There's no point in blasting away at something. You don't use a sledgehammer to crack a walnut do you? So that's the theory behind that. I just try to keep it as simple as possible. I think the art of being a really good drummer is keeping it nice and straight, so it just sits nicely. Tempo fluctuates no matter who you are. Some are worse than others but everyone fluctuates. Other than that, the most important things are keeping it simple and feeling the song. After all, the drummer is only the fourth or fifth member of the band."

Cozy seemed humbler here regarding his position in a band than he perhaps was when with Rainbow. That said, Rainbow and Whitesnake aren't really musically comparable for a whole host of reasons so it probably makes sense not to over think things here and just revel in the wonder of Powell's ability to give the music what it needed.

Moody finished the recording of *Slide It In*. The album was eventually produced by Martin Birch due to Kramer being dismissed by the band for not being what they wanted. There were also personal disagreements between Moody and Coverdale around this time. As Moody was quoted in issue 34 of *Hard Roxx* in 1997; "Me and David weren't friends and co-writers anymore. David never said anything to me. He just didn't socialise with me anymore. David was a guy who five, six years earlier was my best friend. Then one night we were in Germany and we did kind of a mini festival with Thin Lizzy and John Sykes was on guitar. Back at the hotel we were all sitting around and David was really talking a lot to John Sykes. I was sitting there quietly and David just turned around to me, pointing his fingers and said, 'Don't you ever turn your back on the audience again'. I went, 'Pardon?' He said, 'That's really unprofessional', in front of John Sykes to make me look small and I thought to myself, 'That's it'. I nearly said to him, 'Get him in the band', 'cos even I knew by then he wanted somebody like John Sykes, 'cos he looked good and he was a good guitar player. I decided to leave after finishing the end of

the tour. The last gig was in Brussels in Belgium in October
'83. After the gig, I said to the tour manager, 'I want to have
a meeting in my room with all the band: I have something
to say'. The other band members arrived and I said, 'Where
is David?' The tour manager came and told me, 'David is
entertaining people in his suite, and he won't come down'."

Bands will be bands. This is essentially just one side of
the story and thus I am quoting Moody cautiously but I think
what he said is relevant in terms of how it demonstrates the
extent of friction in the band, at least according to Moody's
experience of it.

Once Moody had left the band, John Sykes was announced
as the new guitarist of Whitesnake. It was at the same time
that it was announced that Colin Hodgkinson had been fired
and was to be replaced on bass by the returning Neil Murray.
As a result of such line-up changes, the UK release of *Slide
It In* features Moody and Hodgkinson on guitar and bass
respectively, whilst the American release of the album has
Sykes and Murray playing those parts. When *Slide It In* was
released in the UK, it did have chart success by getting to
number nine but was strongly criticised for the innuendo in its
lyrics. It is rumoured that this was a factor in the decision to
remix the album for its release into the American market but it
seems equally plausible that it was due to the line-up changes
in the band. The American version of the album was produced
by Keith Olsen.

Essentially, Whitesnake's line-up changed even during the
making of just one album. It's not unheard of with a band line-
up but when you consider how many people came and went in
such a short space of time, it probably wasn't the smoothest of
positions for Cozy to be involved with. Disappointing really
considering that Cozy appeared enthusiastic about joining
the band. He was quoted in *Kerrang!* in June 1983; "It's nice
to be with a stable group like Whitesnake. It's a pleasure to

play with them. There's a lot of energy there and that's what this kind of music is all about, energy and spontaneity. Some bands spend months in the studio going through it bar by bar. But that's not what it's all about!"

When asked about public opinion on him joining Whitesnake, Cozy was quoted; "I've been delighted. I expected a rough ride because there'd been a lot of adverse press about what I'd been doing. But I went down fabulously well and it was very touching to hear the number of kids who gave me a round of applause. I thought I was going to get a lot of flak from them, but it was the journalists, not the kids, who really put the knife in and started twisting. When I won the *Kerrang!* poll it made me feel much better. I don't mind touring, I'm a workaholic, like Phil Collins, though I don't do as many sessions as I used to." (Cozy's mentioning of the adverse press refers to negative comments made in the press about him leaving and joining so many bands. As much as the phrase is probably after Cozy's time, hater's gonna hate and all that).

In the same article, Cozy was quoted in a way that suggests that he had a sense of humour about being so in demand at the time; "I don't know what it is. Perhaps it's because they like the cigars I smoke or the bottle of gin I bring with me to sessions."

The band toured Europe with the line-up of Coverdale, Sykes, Galley, Murray, Lord and of course, Powell. More turbulence ensued. Guitarist Mel Galley had an accident at a fairground in Germany that damaged some of the nerves in his arm; it resulted in him not being able to play guitar but Coverdale kept him on as a member of the band. The tour continued and by April 1984 the reunion of Deep Purple Mk2 was looming. As a result, it was on 16th April 1984 at the Grand Hotel, Stockholm that Jon Lord played his last concert with Whitesnake before leaving to go back to Deep Purple.

Jon Lord's last performance with Whitesnake happened to be recorded as this gig was filmed for the Swedish TV show, *Måndagsbörsen*. Richard Bailey was brought in to replace Jon Lord and the band was signed up to open up for acts in America that included Quiet Riot and Dio. Whitesnake's last show of the tour was at the *Rock In Rio* festival in Brazil. Oh and Galley was fired by Coverdale after talking in an interview about plans to reform Trapeze (there's that Deep Purple connection again... Glenn Hughes was in Trapeze prior to joining Deep Purple Mk3 around the time that Coverdale joined the band).

Dramas, hirings and firings aside, The American leg of the *Slide It In* tour had been very well received and had resulted in the album getting a lot of radio play. There was an increasing demand for Whitesnake in America. By supporting Quiet Riot and Dio, both of which were already doing well in America by that point, Whitesnake were able to raise their profile. MTV was a big promotional vehicle for many bands at the time and Whitesnake's videos for their songs 'Slow An' Easy' and 'Love Ain't No Stranger' all contributed towards the band becoming absolutely massive in America with the eponymous album that would be released three years later in 1987.

David Coverdale was quoted in June 2001 in *Classic Rock* where he explained how the events of 1984 were somewhat of a catalyst that led to him ultimately cracking America in 1987; "I didn't really work America in '84, I had broken all attendance records and merchandise records in Europe but I still lost three grand. My marriage was in tatters and then David Geffen called up and said, 'It is about time that you took America seriously.' There was nothing to keep me in London — so, rather than taking potshots at America from across the pond, I decided to relocate, and had an extraordinary four or five years."

Cozy was quoted in July 1986 in *Kerrang!*; "The last

gig I did was with Whitesnake in Rio (January 1985) and I still can't understand why it all fell apart, but that's the way this business goes. There were any number of personal and business problems which weren't resolved. I'm not known for being particularly patient with people who say they're gonna do things and then don't deliver. I give everything when I play and I expect the band to give the same amount of enthusiasm. If they don't, then I'm gone. It's the same with every band I've been in, and I've probably not made many friends by doing that. But I figure you get value for money if you get me in a band!"

A good point from Mr Powell there as in, regardless of the politics of all the bands he was ever in, there is no denying that he added a lot of musical quality to each of them. All of the musicians mentioned in this chapter have made such an important contribution to music in the last fifty years or so; there is certainly no intention on my part to represent any of them in a derogatory light. That said, when looking back at all of the personnel related instability that Cozy was witness to during his days with Whitesnake, there's definitely that feeling of, "best off out of that one Cozy!"

In February 1988 in *Kerrang!*, Cozy was quoted; "I was asked to carry on with Whitesnake and was offered a deal which I didn't think was competitive so I said no. I chose to leave and go with ELP. Since then Whitesnake have sold out in my opinion. They've gone from a hard rock blues band to a heavy metal glam rock outfit. It's been a great success and you can't take anything away from that. David Coverdale is a great singer. The fact that I left was purely business, and he's got a great drummer now with Tommy Aldridge. I wish them all good luck and I've got no axe to grind. David has done really well and selling seven million albums can't be bad!"

The era of Whitesnake that coincides with Cozy's stint in the band is quite a frustrating one to consider the more I think about it as in, there was so much talent in that band. Looking at it with a revisionist historian hat on, it makes me think "come on guys! Get it together and stop wasting all that energy on politics and fallings out." But I guess that's bands for you and in fairness, Whitesnake is not the exception in such regard. Also, sometimes frustration perhaps needs to be there as a catalyst for change; this era of Whitesnake was certainly pivotal for David Coverdale going on to crack the American market in a big way. The *Slide It In* album did well enough commercially but the friction in the band at the time was such that it does leave one wondering what more could have been achieved with the musical potential of the line-up, had they all just got on a bit better at the time. By 1985, Coverdale and Sykes had started working on material for the next Whitesnake album. Cozy had left for Emerson, Lake and Powell.

Sometimes I get the impression that for as many sources that stipulate that Whitesnake and indeed Deep Purple were full of egos, Jon Lord often seemed to come across as one of the nice guys of rock in how he spoke well of his colleagues in interviews. In April 1999 in *Classic Rock*, Lord was quoted regarding his memories of Powell; "He (Cozy) played on my solo album, *Before I Forget*, on a track featuring the recorder, after which the drums came thundering in. Even for Cozy it was rather tricky, and he did it stunningly. I think what really concerned him was that Simon Phillips was playing on another song and he wanted to be the best. But Cozy would always do you a favour whether he'd known you for fifty years or fifty minutes. Once, when I was moving house, he turned up on my doorstep with Mel Galley and said, 'Now listen here, Brigadier, (that was Cozy's nickname for Jon Lord during the Whitesnake days) there's absolutely no need to call these removal chappies. We'll do it together!' Naturally, I paid him the going rate, which was as much Gordon's gin and tonic as he could get down him!"

Throughout this chapter, I'm cautious that it doesn't portray Whitesnake in the best light on the basis of the in-fighting and personnel changes when Cozy was in the band. I'm sure it was just bad luck for all of those concerned. I doubt that anybody sets up a band with the intention of having a hard time of it.

Before Cozy Powell was even in Whitesnake, David Coverdale was quoted in September 1980 in *Cash Box* regarding his experiences in Deep Purple who he was with from 1973 through to 1976; "I experienced extremes in every fashion. I went through a lot, and I'm glad that I did. I learned how to take care of myself and that you can't equate making money with having a good time. Purple was a great group until it became five ego maniacs fighting for the spotlight."

It wouldn't be fair to say that whilst Powell was in Whitesnake, the problems were predominantly down to something that Coverdale was or wasn't doing; that wouldn't be fair at all. Besides, just because the *Slide It In* album didn't really get the success it deserved until 1987 (it's a good album, give it a listen, Cozy's drumming is great on it), it doesn't mean that it was entirely panned when it was released. It could also be considered that it had a hard act to follow what with the success of the previous Whitesnake album.

Also, when Powell joined Whitesnake, he seemed optimistic about how everyone in the band was capable of being professional as a result of being experienced in the music industry. He was quoted in *Kerrang!* in June 1983; "I then joined Michael who went through a rather hard time for a few months and didn't know if he was coming or going. I left but there's no animosity. The good thing about Whitesnake is that we've all been around for a long time so we don't need arguments. There's constructive criticism, but not punch-ups." Evidently, it seems that when Cozy joined Whitesnake, both him and Coverdale went into the whole thing with the intention of keeping things running smoothly on a personnel basis. They probably didn't quite achieve it but still.

In later interviews, Cozy was quoted on his reasons for leaving Whitesnake. In February 1988 in *Metal Hammer*; "The deal I was offered (with Whitesnake) wasn't exactly the one agreed on between David (Coverdale) and I. So I stuck out for what I thought was right and David for what he thought was right — and as he was the boss he won. For me it was either take it or leave it... and I left, it was simple as that. ELP came along, and musically, it was very tempting, to be following someone like Carl Palmer, a very fine player and very well respected."

In *Kerrang!* in June 1983; "People assumed I'd left the (Michael Schenker) group and now they ask how long I'm going to stay with Whitesnake. But look at Aynsley Dunbar. He's been in eight bands in five years. If I join a band it's because I enjoy the music. If, eventually, there's a lot of behind the scenes friction, the position changes."

In *Hit Parade* in September 1985; "I'm not happy that Whitesnake cut my drum solo out of some of the gigs. We're playing nearly an hour and a half. Can't they give me a shot? I love the guys, and the music, but I do feel the need to step out a little." It's a disappointment to observe that Cozy felt that way about his time in Whitesnake, especially seeing that, when he joined, he expressed so much enthusiasm on what he wanted to bring to the band. Cozy was quoted in *Kerrang!* in June 1983; "The reason I do solos is because the kids like them. Mine is short, sweet and has lots of effects. It's very spectacular. I'm not trying to sell my drumming, though. I do it in the show, but most of the time I act as the band's driver. I try to keep the band together and, in fact, I wanted to drop the solo when I joined Whitesnake, but David said I had to do one production number. I can only play one way. Flat out."

In the same interview, Cozy was quoted; "I wanted to get

myself fit again so we (Cozy and Coverdale) went on a sort of Commando course (in Dartmoor). It did us a lot of good. When you're sleeping rough in tents, you tend to come down to earth rather sharpish. I did most of the cooking. I had to do everything, actually. David is not the most outdoor person I've ever met! The tracks are already sounding good, a bit like the stuff on the *Come An' Get It* album. We've been rehearsing at Jon Lord's place and we're all very happy with things. It's nice for me. For the first time in seven years I can just play drums instead of having to try and run the show. David is such a positive person — he knows exactly what he wants. I just go in and play and don't have to worry about things happening. Right now we're working on a few surprises for Donington because that's going to be a very big gig for us. I want to make sure we have a few spectacular surprises because this will be the first time I've been there since headlining with Rainbow. We want to make it a show to remember. People wearing pacemakers will be advised not to attend."

Chapter Eight:
Emerson, Lake & Powell (1985–1986)

Emerson, Lake and Powell is sometimes abbreviated to ELPowell or ELP2 as a variant on the band's original name and members; Keith Emerson, Greg Lake and Carl Palmer. Emerson, Lake and Powell released one eponymous studio album in 1986. The debut single from the album, 'Touch And Go', peaked at number sixty on the Billboard charts on 19th July of the same year.

Some sources seem to imply that on a personal level, Cozy's time in Emerson, Lake and Powell was often peppered with disagreements and conflict. All three of the artists in this chapter are no longer with us so in the name of being ethical here, there is no way I am going to speculate on gossip relating to personal fallings out. That's not fair on those concerned. Why do that when there is a fascinating and worthwhile musical legacy to be discussed. All three musicians made a phenomenal contribution to music, both as individuals and collectively.

When Cozy joined the band that would become known as Emerson, Lake and Powell, musically it was arguably a more demanding time for him. Up until that point in his career, although he had played across a range of styles and genres, hard rock and heavy metal had been the main thing. Emerson and Lake were massive contenders in the progressive rock genre and working with them was an excellent vehicle for Cozy to demonstrate his drumming talents in a way that artistically, added something new to his CV. Cozy had excelled in his work with Rainbow and had a fantastic reputation as a very capable and heavy drummer by then. Working with Emerson and Lake was seemingly a creatively constructive time for Powell.

Cozy was quoted in July 1986 in *Kerrang!*; "I've had to work hard with them (Emerson and Lake), learning a lot of the old stuff. It's not just a three minute twelve-bar blues you have to learn. It's been interesting working out on *Tarkus*. It's opened up my musical vocabulary. They are clever pieces of music and Keith isn't exactly a three-chord wonder. He comes up with some very clever stuff, and Greg as well. I've had to learn 'Pirates' (from *Works Volume One*) which runs for fourteen minutes. They are also playing *Pictures At An Exhibition*, it's not three choruses, verse and fade out. To play this stuff you need a lot of experience and confidence. It's not beginner's music, that's for sure. It's been a real challenge and it's brought me out from being a backing drummer, which I was in Michael Schenker Group and Whitesnake. I can express myself now and play a solo as well! So I've been practising hard and I've even stopped drinking, which a lot of people can't believe. I am determined to make this successful, I'm going to give it my best shot because the band is worthy of a good crack."

After taking part in the Phenomena project and assisting in the formation of Blue Murder, in 1986 Cozy Powell teamed up with Emerson and Lake (Cozy was quoted in *Kerrang!* in February 1988 on his explanation of not sticking with Blue Murder; "My project with Blue Murder broke down because they wanted me to sign a five year contract, which was far too long and restricting for me.").

Cozy was quoted retrospectively in April 1999 in *Classic Rock*; "People said, 'You only got in because your name starts with a P', but the guy they had before me was called Tony

Beard! Funnily enough though, the guy before him was Simon Phillips! But it was great, possibly the most enjoyable part of my career. But Greg and Keith fell out again and it all ended in litigation!"

In the same article, Keith Emerson was quoted; "I remember Cozy being in my barn in Sussex. He set up his impressive drum rig, then realised he had no drumsticks! He considered using some fallen branches from by the orchard until a local farmer drove into town to get some proper ones. They weren't the correct weight but were sufficient when he held them upside down using the fat end. Then he'd do his drum solo and it would be like World War III had broken out."

Cozy was quoted in July 1986 in *Kerrang!*; "The Whitesnake situation was very hectic and we did a lot of American touring. The last tour finished it off really. The aggravations were brought to a head on that little jaunt. I parted company with them and came onto the musical transfer list again. I didn't know whether to take another sabbatical or whether to carry on. Then a phone call came through saying that Keith and Greg wanted someone to come down and help them do an album. They had already tried two or three drummers, apparently. I've known Keith for years anyway, and he said, 'Come on down and have a blow.' I had just got back from Rio and I went down to his house only to find I'd left my sticks at home. I felt a right prat!"

Also, "When I arrived they realised I could do the job onstage as well. It all worked and we get on very well. I really enjoy the music anyway. It wasn't the only offer I had at the time. I could have done a number of other things, but obviously when you get the chance to work with musicians of that calibre, you take it. I've been with guitar-based bands for ten years, so it was nice to get into a keyboards trio. I've always wanted to work with a trio ever since I saw Ginger Baker years ago with Cream."

In 1985, Emerson and Lake had the intention of reforming the original ELP line-up with Carl Palmer. However, drummer Palmer wasn't able to commit due to other contractual obligations that he held at the time. A number of drummers were auditioned before Powell. The band always stipulated that Cozy's surname conveniently beginning with the letter P was coincidental rather than what qualified him to drum for them. In July 1986 in *Keyboard*, the band joked about having wanted to approach "Gene Prupa", "Phil Pollins" and "Ringo Parr" for the job prior to Powell. During the recording of Emerson, Lake and Powell's album, a tractor had accidentally crashed into Keith Emerson's barn studio; it resulted in some parts of the album needing to be recorded again.

In the same article, he joked of the band's name, "Perhaps we should have called it "Emerson, Lake and Plow"."

In July 1986 in *Kerrang!*, Cozy was quoted; "I went in the snow to Sussex where Keith lives and began working on material. Then Keith said, 'Do you fancy having a bash through 'Fanfare For The Common Man'?' We started playing, one thing led to another and the next thing I knew they'd asked me to join! It seemed that Keith had done a load of film soundtracks, and Greg had made a couple of solo albums and been on tour with Gary Moore since ELP first split, and they were just going to make an album together called Emerson & Lake. Nothing more sinister than that. When I arrived on the scene they began to think, 'This guy can perform, there's a possibility of getting a band together here.' Then everybody started saying, 'Oh, Cozy has only got it because his last name starts with a P.' It's just a coincidence that I have the same initials as Carl Palmer, I don't get jobs on the strength of my initials, I get them because of the way I play! They could have booked Carl Perkins for that matter, although he might have had difficulty getting round a drum kit! After all the furore died down, we decided to get on with the work. I didn't want to copy Carl Palmer's style, I wanted to sound like me. You know our styles well enough to know the difference between us. I go in there, bang, do my stuff and let the album speak for itself."

Cozy clearly had a good sense of humour about the P thing. He was quoted in May 1986 in *Billboard*; "When we started recording last year, I told them that if they'd wanted somebody whose name started with a P, there were a lot of other drummers who might have fit in better. I can think of guys like Jeff Porcaro, Simon Phillips or Neil Peart but they obviously wanted another C.P."

The summer of 1986 seems like it featured some fascinating collaborations that many considered unlikely. In the July *Kerrang!* that features the interview with Cozy, there was also a feature on the *Monsters Of Rock* tour for that year including the parody rock band, Bad News from *The Comic Strip Presents…* It's fascinating what people will regard as an unlikely pairing when actually, by the time Cozy had joined ELP, he had very much proved himself to be a fantastic and very capable drummer earlier in his career.

It is evident that the E and L of ELP were keen to welcome Cozy Powell into the band. Greg Lake was quoted on the matter in August 1986 in the *Fort Worth Star — Telegram*; "The fact is, Cozy is a tremendous player and a tremendous live performer. And it was the fact that he had this added ability of being a great onstage performer that made him perfect for the role. Keith and I decided to make an album together about two years ago, and we started with a concept of basically writing some music together and making an album with a selection of different musicians on sort of a session basis. We wrote some of the music and got part way along the path of doing it. But we said, 'Look, the first person we need is a drummer', Carl was in Asia. But, in any event, I think Keith and I felt that we would welcome some fresh input. We started to play with a few different drummers, and then Cozy Powell became available. We asked Cozy if he'd like to play some sessions on the record, and he said he'd love to. Once we started to work with him, it became obvious that the band had the potential to come back as a three-piece and be very, very strong. So, at that point, instead of a Keith Emerson/Greg Lake album, it became an Emerson, Lake and Powell album. Keith and I felt the time was right. We definitely welcomed the camaraderie of being involved in a group as opposed to this life as a solo artist, which tends to be rather lonely. We actually enjoy working together in a group. Towards the end of the days of Emerson, Lake and Palmer, I think we probably had toured just too much. We had been on the road for nine years doing two hundred days a year. And it became too much for us. We just became tired of doing it. At that point, we felt enough was enough. But, like anything, absence makes the heart grow fonder. Because of the time away from it, it became an attractive thing again... to go out on the road and to enjoy the life of being in a group."

In the same article, Lake was quoted on his philosophy about why the original ELP had decided to call it a day; "To a certain extent, I think every group has a fairly turbulent type of ongoing situation. In anything in which people care deeply and passionately about what they do, everyone has an opinion. If you care a lot, there are bound to be conflicts from time to time over what gets done and how it gets done. But I don't think it was from an egocentric base. With us, it was never a petty-argument-type thing ever. We never intended it to break up in the sense that we all fell out and never wanted to work together again. We just simply couldn't face doing another tour or making another album at that stage of our career."

It is exciting to consider that Cozy Powell was involved in the comeback of a band that many fans were pleased about. Lake added; "We had no way of knowing what sort of reception we'd have, but we're obviously very happy about the way things have gone. We're very grateful that we've still got that many fans out there who are still keen to see and hear the group. We're just very happy about it."

The album featured music that was typical of ELP's established style; long progressive rock suites and mellow ballads, often with a classical theme. The track 'Mars, The Bringer Of War' is a piece that was originally composed by Gustav Holst. Greg Lake had performed it previously during his time with King Crimson. On the song, 'The Score', lyrics are quoted from ELP's *Brain Salad Surgery* album.

Additionally, in Emerson, Lake and Powell's live performances, the set list included material from the original Emerson, Lake and Palmer repertoire. Bootlegs exist of studio rehearsals and live recordings of Emerson, Lake and Powell. Luckily, such material was released officially in 2003 under the title, *The Sprocket Sessions*.

Cozy's drumming in the live shows was just as exciting as his '1812 Overture' solo when he was in Rainbow. Cozy was quoted in July 1986 in *Kerrang!* as he talked about his drum solo in the Emerson, Lake and Powell live shows; "I'm doing 'Mars, The Bringer Of War' as a featured number. Funnily enough, I did that to a backing tape with Whitesnake, so when I brought it along Keith said he'd like to play it himself. He learnt it in a few minutes. Makes you sick doesn't it! Why use a tape when Keith can play it? I'll be doing that onstage with all the usual Powell idiocy — that's where the pyro (pyrotechnics) comes in. More and more over the top. I don't know whether I'll survive this drum solo. If you read that half of Texas has been wiped out, you'll know the pyro went wrong! It gets more dangerous every year. We put out a warning over the PA for anybody with a dangerous heart condition... We're doing a good cross-section of stuff, and now we can make it sound even more exciting because of the technology available. Keith has got a load of computer stuff and it's quite amazing the sound that three people can make these days. It's fantastic. And the special effects we've got have never been seen before anywhere in the world. Things have been built for this tour that will be unique."

In his interview in July 1986 in *Kerrang!*, Powell considered that Emerson, Lake and Powell had been welcomed more in the USA than the UK. He felt that this applied not only in terms of the band's formation but also in terms of how their album and live tours were received, particularly by the media. Cozy was quoted; "A lot of people have said, 'Well, why do it (ELP) again?' The reason is simple: because it's a new band. I've brought in a load of ideas and Keith and Greg have been all fired up again. We're gonna put on a show that's gotta be seen to be believed. ELP were always noted for being outrageous and that's gonna be the policy now... As soon as the band came back it was greeted with total press derision in this country (UK) and absolute uproar everywhere else. America has gone potty about it. The album — as we speak — is twenty-eight in the Billboard charts within four weeks, and every major magazine is interested in us. And yet over here ELP is a dirty word. I just don't know why. None of the reviews (except in *Kerrang!*) talked about the music, they just criticised the individuals. We weren't sulking, we just thought, 'What is the point of talking to anybody?'"

The Emerson, Lake and Powell album certainly appears to have been met with enthusiasm in the American press of the day. In May 1986, *Billboard* reported that the album "is guaranteed to command strong radio play". The eponymous album was reviewed in *Billboard* in May 1986; "With veteran drummer Cozy Powell replacing Carl Palmer, this British art/rock trio picks up where it left off in the seventies. Keith Emerson's keyboard orchestrations offer epic scale while Greg Lake's hearty vocals handle the melodic hooks. AOR will embrace their return, starting with 'Touch And Go'."

The band's tour (which was sponsored by Westwood One Radio Networks and Coca-Cola USA — that stuff gets everywhere!) began on the 15th August 1986 in El Paso, Texas and initially, sixty-five dates were set up for as far as late October. Disappointingly, Emerson, Lake and Powell's live tour was impaired by disagreements with the management, resulting in the band firing them. The difficulties snowballed from there and ultimately, the band broke up. Cozy was quoted on the matter in *Metal Hammer* in February 1988; "With both Whitesnake and ELP, it was nothing to do with the music but totally to do with the contractual side. And that's why I'm no longer with either of them."

Cozy offered further insight into how he approached ELP both musically and personally when he was quoted in *Rhythm* in October 1987; "I came to the situation looking forward to playing the music. It took me a while to work out some of the stuff, but I didn't want to play like Carl Palmer, nor am I that kind of drummer anyway. What I did was to simplify it, if you like, and make it more powerful. If you can imagine *Tarkus* with two bass drums instead of one then you'd think it possibly had more flow. That's arguable but unless you'd seen the two of us each playing together, you wouldn't really be able to tell how it all compared. The main point is that you could still recognise the tunes even though obviously there was something different happening in the rhythm section."

Also; "I think where ELP was concerned, the album was a bit stiff. We took so long over it and should have done it spontaneously, as opposed to working out every beat. Still, it's easy to be clever after the event. I was disappointed when it all fell apart, but when Emerson and Lake decided they'd fell out for the fifteenth million time, I'd had enough. It was a shame that it ended as a bit of a farce where the right hand didn't know what the left hand was doing. And as usual, the drummer got left in the middle of it all! The trouble was that no one in England saw the live shows we did in America which went down very well. You know, we were selling out big arenas — twenty-six thousand in New York. The show was well put together, very well paced and entertaining. It was very visual, all the usual stuff including the daggers going into the keyboards."

On playing 'Mars, The Bringer Of War' live, Cozy was quoted in the same feature in *Rhythm*; "I've always tried to make the solo a bit of a production, always tried to do things differently. This time I had all these effects — artillery noises and machine guns, shells exploding and bombs going off. We were using a quadraphonic PA which nobody has really done since (Pink) Floyd. So between all this gear I managed to produce the effect of a war going on in the auditorium. You know, a bomb over here, an explosion there, the sound of a plane flying from one speaker to the other. With all the flames and lighting effects, it was pretty impressive... I certainly enjoyed playing all that stuff. My playing is all about making it spectacular."

Keith Emerson went on to work with Carl Palmer with the addition of Robert Berry in 1988. Cozy went on to do a short stint with Gary Moore. It didn't last long. Cozy's musical CV was about to grow further with another high-profile band, Black Sabbath.

Chapter Nine:
Black Sabbath
(1988–1991, 1994–1995)

C ozy had just finished his work with Cinderella in 1988 on their *Long Cold Winter* album. It took some persuading to get him to join Black Sabbath but such was Tony Iommi's enthusiasm for Cozy's drumming. Cozy was quoted retrospectively in April 1999 in *Classic Rock* as he spoke of his reluctance to join the band; "I thought they'd had one personnel change too many, but *Headless Cross* was a successful album."

It sounds like one of those things where in this case, the power of hindsight makes someone glad they took an opportunity that they were tempted to reject.

Around the time of working with Black Sabbath, they were not Cozy's only commitment. He worked with Gary Moore in 1988, Black Sabbath between 1988 and 1991 and then again between 1994 and 1995. During 1992 and 1993, Powell started a touring band - Cozy Powell's Hammer, as he had done for his solo work in the seventies. Cozy also toured with Brian May in 1993. The significance of all of this is that whilst Cozy's contribution to Black Sabbath was of key importance to both the band and his own career, it was not the only project he was involved in at the time. As ever, Cozy was a versatile, capable and independent musician.

By the time Cozy joined Black Sabbath, the band had

their own legacy and one that was well established. His first album with them was their fourteenth one, *Headless Cross*. It was released on 24th April 1989. It was the second of Black Sabbath's albums to feature Tony Martin on vocals.

The way that the *Headless Cross* album came to be is a story of change and challenge; prior to the recording of the album, Black Sabbath were without a record label. Tony Iommi recalled of the situation in his 2012 autobiography, *Iron Man*, that after an eighteen-year partnership, the band had been dropped by Warner Bros. Records in 1988. The band had also been dropped by Vertigo Records in the UK by this point.

It was when Iommi met Miles Copeland, owner of IRS Records that he was told by him; "You know how to write albums, you know what people want. You do it and I'm fine with it." In his autobiography, Iommi recalls how being given such creative and indeed commercial freedom confirmed his decision to sign the band to IRS. Contextually, it is plausible that whilst Cozy had less involvement in such negotiations, being invited to join a high-profile band that was undergoing a period of creative rejuvenation was a promising prospect, especially for Cozy with his ability to contribute to the writing of new material, as he had done in his previous engagements.

In April 1989, *Cash Box* reported that "*Headless Cross*, Sabbath's new LP, may signify a real comeback for the group." There definitely seemed to be the theme of a band comeback underlining the *Headless Cross* album. When it was reviewed in June 1989 in *Billboard*, it was stated; "On its IRS debut, Iommi's venerable British group takes another stab at reclaiming an audience now hooked on Sab-influenced outfits. Now there's a generation that probably thinks the only person Ozzy Osbourne ever sang with is Lita Ford, the timing could be right. Lead singer Tony Martin is more in the vein of Ronnie James Dio than Osbourne, especially on tunes such as

'When Death Calls' and the title track."

Yep, definitely a strong theme of Black Sabbath making a comeback. It was stated in the *Headless Cross* tour programme; "After a three-year hiatus, Black Sabbath explode back into action with *Headless Cross* — the new album which some critics say is their best. A massive world tour and a new definitive line-up... Iommi has recruited the services of hard rock veteran drummer Cozy Powell. Powell has worked with the best in rock over a long career. His no nonsense powerhouse drumming is the perfect foundation for the Sabs. The final piece of the jigsaw is the highly experienced Neil Murray. Neil, who partnered Cozy in Whitesnake, adds dimension to the rhythm section and his soaring bass runs again make the perfect foil for Iommi. As you can see this is a line-up to be taken seriously indeed... This marks the dawn of an exciting era and Sabbath's third decade in the realms of rock 'n' roll, a feat not many groups can stake claim to. There is no doubt the Sabs are back with a vengeance."

It was in April 1989 in *Cash Box* that Powell was quoted as having said, "We've got the best unknown singer, we think, that's come along for quite a number of years. He tells stories in the way he writes his lyrics — he's naturally perfect for the Sabbath image. Tony (Iommi) and I have gone back a long time, over twenty years. We'd known each other back in the old days, when Sabbath was first put together. I was asked to join the band a while back, actually and because of other commitments, I couldn't do it. We decided this time 'round that the name of Sabbath has been much maligned over the years, and it was time to start again with a fresh slate and do it properly. The management's completely changed, we have a new record company, and the album was put together relatively quickly. We co-produced it, Tony and I, and we worked very hard on trying to establish Black Sabbath as a force to be reckoned with again."

Powell further enthused about the band's new record company, "A lot of record companies had a chance to sign us (post Warner Bros.) but the only company that really wanted us to make a proper Black Sabbath record was IRS, and Miles Copeland. He just said, 'look, you just gotta make me a record that I can say is a Black Sabbath record. I don't want a three-minute single. We don't want you to sell out in any way, we just want you to make a great record', he was very supportive of us."

I think this is an excellent quote from Cozy as in, it is demonstrative of what he was about as an artist; whilst he could play ball as a session musician and go on *Top of The Pops* with 'Dance With The Devil', he was capable of so much more than the typical commercial restrictions that he was keen to go against - his time in this period of Black Sabbath certainly seemed suggestive of that.

In the same article, Tony Iommi was quoted, "We don't understand why, but a record company signs Black Sabbath, or whoever, and then they try to change it — want 'em to sound like Foreigner, or whoever it might be. That's what was happening. In Miles Copeland, we found — finally — somebody who wanted us, without change, to do a Black Sabbath album exactly as we see. Let's face it, it's only the group itself that knows how it should be. No young upstart can come along and say, 'Well, this is how Black Sabbath is', because you know you started the thing and you should play as you know how to do it."

Tony Martin was quoted in *Sounds* in May 1989 as he explained the inspiration for the album, "Headless Cross is a village in the Midlands. I used to live there. It can be a pretty eerie place." Typical Black Sabbath when you consider the mood of their very first album (that one with the scary looking woman on the cover art where the music apparently scared the shit out of lots of people due to never having heard anything like it before).

Iommi and Powell began writing the songs for the *Headless Cross* album in Iommi's home. Tony Martin joined them for rehearsals. Iommi was considering asking Ronnie James Dio back into the band as vocalist but Cozy persuaded him to stick with Tony Martin. Powell and Iommi decided to produce the album themselves, again, another creative freedom afforded to them by the laid-back approach of the IRS record label.

Cozy really made his mark on *Headless Cross*. Laurence Cottle played bass on the album as a session musician but was not officially a member of the band, even though he did appear in the video for the album's title track. He wasn't however, featured in any of the band's promotional photos. For the tour of the album, Neil Murray played bass. On the album, Brian May did the guitar solo in the middle of the song, 'When Death Calls'. What a small world the music industry is! This is probably something that went in Cozy's favour from as far back as his days with RAK (I'm not negating his talent here, not even slightly but as ever, with a lot of these things it's a question of who you know isn't it. Industry related networking and all that).

Cozy was a significant part of Black Sabbath's history as a band, for they were one of the first to tour in Russia in 1989 after Mikhail Gorbachev had lifted restrictions on acts from the west being allowed into the country. The band played a total of twenty-five shows there; thirteen of which were at Moscow's Olympic Hall and twelve of which were at EKS Hall in Leningrad. The afternoon and evening shows were filmed on 19th November for official release. The footage eventually made it to DVD in 2008 (it's really good viewing, well worth a look; a strong example of how versatile Cozy was as a musician who had played across a range of styles with so many different bands by this point in his career).

Headless Cross scored some excellent reviews. It was

considered by many to be representative of Black Sabbath taking an excellent new direction. As a band renowned for many line-up changes and all kinds of dramas, some of Black Sabbath's previous albums had been panned as being a bit "same old, same old". Perhaps people were bored of the tried and tested formula and the way in which the longevity of the band made it seem like something of an institution. However, that really did change with *Headless Cross* in 1989.

In April 1989, *Cash Box* reviewed the album; "Heavy moods, heavy power, trudging along like a giant snowplough. Yep, Black Sabbath gets it together again, better than they've been in a long, long time." It was also reviewed in July 1989 in *Music And Media*; "The band that are widely credited as the inventors of heavy metal are back with a really captivating album. High pitched vocals, heavy guitars and an undoubted stadium appeal are the main ingredients here. Gloomy tracks like 'Devil And Daughter', 'Nightwing' and 'Headless Cross' are particularly outstanding."

Headless Cross stayed in the Billboard 200 chart for eight weeks. It peaked at number 115. As was reported in August 1990 in *Music And Media*, "In the last year, Black Sabbath has been one of IRS's best-selling acts in continental Europe; their LP, *Headless Cross*, has sold 250,000 copies."

The sales in America were low which ultimately resulted in the truncation of the tour there. However, I would strongly urge anyone in doubt of the impact of *Headless Cross* to note that the reviews of the album itself were largely positive, particularly in view of the band's albums prior to it. Better still, listen to the album. It has some beautiful riffs that are both heavy and melodic and importantly, Cozy's drumming adds depth and character to every track on the album. In such regard, I advocate that what Cozy did for Black Sabbath's *Headless Cross* album is as artistically and indeed technically monumental as what he contributed to the *Rainbow Rising* album in 1976. Significantly, Cozy has writing credits on all but one of the *Headless Cross* album's tracks.

Cozy's second album with Black Sabbath was the 1990, *Tyr*. The album departed from the darker themes of the lyrics featured on *Headless Cross* and moved more towards something completely different. In his 2012 autobiography, Iommi considered, "for our next album, *Tyr*, we went back to the Woodcray Studios in February 1990, with me and Cozy producing it again. On *Headless Cross*, Tony (Martin) had just come into the band and he assumed, 'oh, Black Sabbath, it's all about the Devil', so his lyrics were full of the Devil and Satan. It was too much in your face. We told him to be a bit more subtle about it, so for *Tyr* he did all these lyrics about Nordic gods and whatnot. It took me a while to get my head around that."

Top points for originality there Black Sabbath! So much so that the *Tyr* album was considered by many to be the most dramatic of changes in terms of the band leaving behind their traditional and established sound in favour of something new. *Tyr* has much reliance on keyboards courtesy of Geoff Nicholls. The music still has a predominantly dark theme to it but again, it's err... different! (go and listen to it, like all good music, it defies description to be honest with you).

It was considered by some that the way the album was mixed was such that Cozy's drums were too loud. I don't think they are. I'm not being biased here either (well, I am a bit because we all are) but the point is this; Cozy's drumming on the album adds a depth and heaviness, much like what his contribution to his first album with Black Sabbath was. Brian May, Ian Gillan and Geezer Butler made guest appearances on the European part of the *Tyr* tour. In particular, May and Butler made guest appearances during the encore of the show at Hammersmith Odeon in London on 8th September 1990.

Cozy has writing credits on all songs on his second album

with Black Sabbath. The album got to number twenty-four in the UK and didn't chart in America, but it did invite interest regarding the originality of it. Both musically and lyrically, it seems to have been met with intrigue.

Cozy was sort of active on Black Sabbath's following album but equally he sort of wasn't. It's a messy one. Basically Black Sabbath released their sixteenth studio album, *Dehumanizer* in June 1992. It was the first Black Sabbath album in over a decade to feature Ronnie James Dio on vocals and drummer Vinny Appice. It was the first time in nine years that the band's original bassist, Geezer Butler, was active again with the band. Cozy was involved with the album but only insofar as working on the initial writing and demo sessions at Rich Bitch Studios in Birmingham. There are bootlegs of these sessions in circulation but essentially, an official release of Cozy's drumming work for this album doesn't exist. Cozy began working on the album and the intention was for him to see the project through to the end. However, in an awkward twist of fate, Cozy broke his pelvic bone in a horse-riding accident, leaving him temporarily immobilised. This resulted in the recruitment of Vinny Appice, who had been Black Sabbath's drummer for the majority of Dio's last stint with the band between 1980 and 1982.

Of course, the unpleasantness of Cozy's accident is a given, but his time with Black Sabbath was terminated for reasons of a more personally uncomfortable nature. Cozy was quoted retrospectively in April 1999 in *Classic Rock*; "Ronnie James Dio had come back in, and he didn't want me. He'd been kicked out of Rainbow and he asked me to play on his solo album to spite Ritchie, but I turned him down. He's hated my guts ever since." Ouch! It's a real shame though considering what Powell and Dio created musically when they were with Rainbow. It's fascinating to wonder what could have been achieved musically in a band line-up consisting of Iommi,

Butler, Dio and Powell. Wow! Sadly, we'll never know.

Cozy teamed up with Black Sabbath once more in 1995 to play on the *Forbidden* album. In September 1995 in Dutch magazine *Aardschok*, Cozy seemed philosophical about the time he felt ousted from the band after his horse-riding accident. He was quoted (be aware that this is translated into English from Dutch); "Tony asked me back himself and that feels good. I was kicked out of the band because a horse fell on top of me and I couldn't play for six months. Also, Tony suddenly ran off with an American version of Black Sabbath. Ronnie James Dio was hired as a singer and he demanded that Vinny Appice was hired as drummer... I was disappointed in Tony's choices and especially so because he didn't want to wait for me to recover. Whether I wanted to play with Dio remains to be seen but I thought Tony (Iommi) was my friend. I was too naive of course; I ought to know better in this business. You learn faster by making mistakes. If I took all disappointments in the music business personally I wouldn't be in it anymore. You just have to remain professional and don't think that you can make friends. They need you or they don't. I have respect for Iommi and the fact that he asked me back himself made me feel good. He said he liked my playing and he thought that I could do something again for Sabbath. Everything had to do with the band, nothing was personal... We think the new album *Forbidden* is the best product up until now because this new/old line-up has to bring Black Sabbath back into the limelight."

It comes across here that Cozy was both candid and yet professional when talking about difficulties with colleagues; certainly a dignified and admirable quality. Equally, there are numerous other articles where Cozy discussed not being pleased with the musical outcome of the *Forbidden* album. The album and the tour both did badly in commercial terms. As ever, the integrity with which Cozy came across in so many interviews certainly adds weight to the theory that he had a straight up, no bullshit kind of approach to things. All the more so perhaps when you consider that so little is known about him on a personal basis. It strikes me that he was very controlled in terms of keeping his private life private whilst not going out of his way to whitewash things when talking about his professional life.

Chapter Ten:
The Brian May Band
(1991-1992, 1993-1994, 1998)

Even before Cozy had joined Black Sabbath, he was in a position of being able to consider his options. He was quoted in *Kerrang!* in February 1988; "Maybe I'll form my own band or join an established band. We'll have to wait and see. I'm going to do some session work, a couple of films scores and an album with Kevin DuBrow, who was with Quiet Riot, another Forcefield album and then I'll sit back and see what comes along. It's the first time in my career I've been free... I've got no immediate plans now but I'm planning to talk to Jack Bruce about forming a new band. Perhaps we'll form the new Cream! That would be nice. I wonder what Ginger Baker is doing now... I want to get into Cream part two. If Eric Clapton and Jack Bruce got together again and couldn't find Ginger, I'd like to be the drummer. That's what I'm interested in doing. That's what it's all about. Otherwise I'd like to come back with a really great new band with the best guitar player and singer around. A Cream II solution is what I'd like to see, there's no bands like that anymore. It's all bullshit, while musicianship has gone out the window, if I can't bring that back, I'll knock it on the head."

It comes across that Powell's priorities may have been based on wanting to make good music whilst knowing his value in the industry.

Having recovered from the accident that was one of many catalysts for him leaving Black Sabbath, Cozy was invited by Brian May, ex-guitarist of Queen, to play in Spain as part of the *Guitar Legends* gig that he was organising. Brian May is probably a musician who needs very little introduction. With Queen he was responsible for more than twenty-two of their top ten hits including 'The Show Must Go On', 'We Will Rock You', 'Who Wants To Live Forever' and 'Hammer To Fall'. May's solo career began in 1991 with the release of *Back To The Light*, his first solo album, along with the single, 'Driven By You'. They were both in the top ten across Europe and sold more than a million copies. Brian was awarded his first Ivor Novello prize as a solo artist based on the success of the single. This all resulted in May undertaking his first solo tour in late 1992. The tour began in South America prior to the USA and then Europe, where the band was a special guest with Guns N' Roses. The band then succeeded to do its own headlining tour that played in North America, Japan and Europe. All tickets were sold for all forty-nine dates during 1993.

On December 4th 1992 Hollywood Records issued a press release; "Queen's legendary guitarist Brian May to kick off first US solo tour opening for Guns N' Roses! Queen's lead guitarist Brian May will embark on his first solo tour of the United States as a special guest for Guns N' Roses in support of his debut solo record, *Back To The Light*, which is already a smash hit in the rest of the world. The long-awaited album is scheduled to be released by Hollywood Records on February 2nd. The song 'Driven By You' is the premier emphasis track to be served to AOR radio. *Back To The Light* features twelve rock tracks containing inspiration and emotion. 'Over these five years, my life and my feelings underwent a catastrophic change and the music reflects the entire process', May revealed. May will begin the Guns N' Roses tour on February 23rd at Erwin Centre in Austin and is scheduled to continue the tour through April. The Brian May Band — including drummer Cozy Powell, bassist Neil Murray, keyboardist Spike Edney, guitarist Mike Casewell, and background singers Chris Thompson, Maggie Ryder and Miriam Stockley — just completed a successful tour of Chile, Argentina, Uruguay and Brazil, Queen's original 1981 stomping ground. 'It's been six years since Queen were last out on the road and there's nothing in the world like it', says May adding, 'I feel this urge to get up there and do something, the same as I did when I was a kid'."

Powell was an asset to Brian May not just musically, but in terms of morale too. May recalled that he was reluctant about embracing a solo career post Queen and advocated that Powell made a tremendously positive difference to his state of mind about the whole thing. May was quoted in *OK!* In June 1998; "I'm a very up-and-down kind of person. I can only work at certain times. I get very depressed, quite often, and Cozy could always lift you out of it. He always made you feel things were worthwhile. He took a great pride in his drumming and really there were very, very few like him. John Bonham was one. A massive, heavy drummer and one of the originators of the style — and Cozy was another."

May was also quoted in *Classic Rock* in April 1999; "It's a cliché but Cozy had always been a hero of mine. Even when I was in Queen, I always thought it would be great to work with him. The first time I was able to do that was at the *Guitar Legends* gig and calling him was a dream come true. Cozy, Neil and myself fitted together perfectly as the nucleus of a band. After Freddie died, Queen had to be considered a non-touring entity. I've always been a very self-questioning person, but Cozy and his optimism were inspirational in helping me find my feet again."

Powell played on the Brian May albums, *Back To The Light* and *Another World*. The song, 'Resurrection' was released as a single. It was written by May, Powell and Jamie Page. It was reviewed in April 1993 in *Billboard*; "Second single from May's solo set, *Back To The Light,* sounds like it could have been recorded by Queen during its heyday. Operatic backing vocals lend appropriate melodrama to a complex, hard rockin' tune. May's slicing, nimble guitar riffs are matched by a thunderous drum solo. Album-rock programmers, take heed."

It could be considered that Cozy Powell was a very important part of a key chapter in Brian May's life, both personally and professionally. In *Guitarist* in July 1998, May was quoted as he elaborated on where he was at with things after Freddie Mercury's passing; "I decided to interact with different people because I thought it would be very good for me. Previously I'd just sit there like a hermit, working on *Made In Heaven* (the fifteenth and final studio album by Queen, released after Freddie Mercury's passing), and I suppose it has a certain intensity because of that. But I felt it was time to start to let stuff in from the outside. So not only did I go out and guest with people, I also made sure that I answered the phone. I had a lot of people ringing me up asking me if I could do this or do that, and I did them all. I had this great influx of input, and every time I did something with another artist, it brought something out from inside me, and sometimes that's been a problem. Now, when someone asks me to write a song about, say, a robot, I go away and do it. From that, I get more inspiration, which becomes another track. When I was writing the album, all these bits came together and I realised what I was trying to do."

It is endearing to think that Cozy was a key part of May's world at such a pivotal and probably emotionally turbulent time.

From late 1992 to early 1993, Cozy Powell's Hammer would tour sporadically. The band consisted of Neil Murray on bass, Mario Parga on guitar and Tony Martin on vocals and occasional guitar. The band toured Europe and made an appearance on TV in Germany. Neil Murray was quoted in *Classic Rock* in April 1999 as he mused on where Cozy may have been at with his relationship with music at the time; "In the last few years, Cozy had to be talked into doing a drum solo. In the 1980s, he'd tried a few other things like '633 Squadron' and 'Mars' from *The Planets Suite* but nothing seemed to work as well as '1812 (Overture)'. In the end I think he became a bit tired of trying to validate his reputation as a showman."

With Neil Murray having worked with Cozy as part of Hammer, Whitesnake, Black Sabbath and the Brian May Band, their professional rapport was such that it was a natural progression for them to join forces with ex-Fleetwood Mac guitarist, Peter Green in 1997.

Cozy's versatility really showed here as Green's blues style of music was far less heavy than what Cozy was more known for. As Green was quoted in *Classic Rock* in April 1999; "It wasn't always thunderous. Many people said that sort of thing, but when Cozy was with me we played many styles of music, so working together wasn't difficult — it was a pleasure."

Peter Green's new band, Splinter Group, was a drop in the ocean in the context of Cozy's career. It wasn't long before Cozy went back to work with Brian May. As Green was quoted in the same article; "My band weren't working on the road at the time, and Cozy had offers to work on some other projects. It was always understood that if a Brian May tour came up, Cozy would do it. When my manager told me about Cozy's death I was stunned."

When Cozy's death was announced in April 1998 in *Music And Media*, it was also mentioned, "Powell was a much respected figure in rock circles, but his recent work with Peter Green emphasised that there was a more sensitive side to his abilities."

The Cozy Powell Story

Cozy's passing away coincided with the recording period of Brian May's second solo album. What should have been a joyous occasion for May was chronically overshadowed by the loss of not only a colleague, but a friend too (the album was released in the June of that year). May was quoted in *Classic Rock* in November 1998 regarding his feelings on the matter at the time; "Cozy was much more than a musician and very much a hero. He wasn't in it for any other reason except that he loved it and he gave it everything. That was his life."

May felt so strongly about what Powell meant to the band that he explained how he was in two minds about whether to carry on with the project (albums and tours) at all after his passing; "I didn't like the idea of going out without Cozy. I thought, 'Well, maybe this is it. Maybe the world is trying to tell me something.' When Freddie went, I really felt strongly that we shouldn't be Queen anymore, and I still think that I don't want to go out around the world with a replacement for Freddie. So that was my first reaction to this. My band was built around Cozy... Then I listened to the album again and I thought that Cozy would want us to take it out on tour. He wouldn't have wanted this album to be swept under the carpet. The best thing is to tour the album proudly and do it for Cozy. So we bit the bullet and auditioned some drummers, and Eric Singer (Kiss, Alice Cooper) walked in and really blew us away. He's phenomenal. It's not going to be like Cozy. Nothing could be like Cozy, but this guy is state-of-the art. He has a bit of that dangerous energy that the Foo Fighters' Taylor Hawkins has. So it will be a new band."

The Hollywood Records press release for May's second album included; "The Brian May Band was formed featuring old friends Cozy Powell on drums, Neil Murray on bass and Spike Edney on keyboards with new friends Jamie Moses on guitar and Shelley Preston and Cathy Porter on backing vocals. The new album, *Another World*, has been three years in the making and sees Brian eager to return to live performance. A UK and European tour again featuring original Brian May Band members Cozy Powell, Neil Murray, Spike Edney and James Moses was planned for autumn this year. At the moment when plans were finalised came the tragic news of Cozy Powell's death in a car crash. Brian and the group were devastated by the loss of Cozy, a brilliant and inspiring musician, crucial contributor to the Brian May album and irreplaceable friend. Plans for the tour are proceeding, but there is yet no decision on who will replace Powell."

It was reported in *Billboard* in September 1998; "Brian May's new solo album, *Another World*, will be released by Hollywood Records September 15th. The album, which has been several years in the making, features Jeff Beck, Taylor Hawkins, and the late drummer Cozy Powell."

Brian May wasn't the only musician whose projects were affected by Cozy's sudden passing. In 1997, Powell was invited by Glenn Tipton of Judas Priest to play on his debut solo album, *Baptism Of Fire*. It was also in late 1997 that Powell worked with Yngwie Malmsteen on his *Facing The Animal* album (Cozy maintained a sense of humour about the similarities between Malmsteen and Blackmore, as he was quoted in fanzine *More Black Than Purple* in August 1997; "He's obviously a Ritchie Blackmore fan. He's got every mannerism that Ritchie's ever done down, but he does it times ten! It's quite weird really. He's copied everything Ritchie does. It's quite amazing.").

In his infinite musical diversity, Cozy also made a record with Zombies singer Colin Blunstone around that time. Cozy had to leave halfway through touring with Malmsteen as a result of a motorcycle injury. Ironically, Cozy was still recovering from such injury when he had his fatal car crash. Notably, some of Cozy Powell's discography consists of posthumous releases. Hardly surprising considering the sizable contribution he made to music throughout his varied and fascinating career.

Chapter Eleven:
Cozy Powell's Solo Projects
Cozy Powell
(1973-1974, 1979-1983, 1992)
Cozy Powell's Hammer
(1974, 1992-1993)

T he term "solo projects" is being used with reservation in this chapter. Whilst all five of Powell's studio albums are in his name, ever the team player, in each of the albums, he fully utilised the talents and ideas of the other musicians who worked with him. His time working with some of the (apparently!) moodiest guitarists in the business served him well in such regard.

Cozy was quoted in November 1984 in *Modern Drummer*; "I think the biggest thing you have to learn is sympathy for other people. You don't just blast through when someone is trying to take a very delicate solo. I think a lot of drummers have a lack of feel in that area. When people start, the first mistake they make is trying to show off, 'look I'm great', I'm sure they are but they just blow through everything everybody else is doing. You've really got to listen very carefully to a guitarist's moods, because their moods usually come out in their playing. Being a drummer you've got to be a) a drummer, b) a psychologist, and who knows what else. It's a combination of things, working with guitarists, I've always found that they're always right, or at least you let them think that they are. Then you turn around and do it the way you want to do it. That's usually the way it is. They're very moody characters, Jeff Beck, Ritchie Blackmore and Michael Schenker are very similar in some respects. They've all got the sort of image they try to keep up. I don't mean Jeff though, he doesn't need an image. He's the best in my book. But Ritchie and Michael tend to try to live up to an image they've created themselves. It's a bit like creating a monster and having to try to live up to it. That's what I've found."

Powell was quoted in *Modern Drummer* in November 1984 as he explained how both his first three solo albums came about; "I was offered a deal on the back of a Rainbow deal. Rainbow had been all over the world. In Japan, for some reason, they love drummers. They seem to really love me and I always seem to win the polls over there. I don't know why, but I do. Also, drummers get more votes than guitarists, bands or anything else. Normally it's guitar players and singers that clean up but it's all different in Japan. So I got the record deal basically because of Japan and the success of Rainbow. It was called *Over The Top* and it featured players like Jack Bruce, Gary Moore and a few others. It sold very well over here and did quite well in Japan so they asked me to do another one. That was called *Tilt*, which Jeff, Gary Moore, Jack and David Sancious played on. *Over The Top* was prior to Michael Schenker and *Tilt* was done while I was with him. When we had a bit of time off, I'd go into the studio and do a couple of tracks. After I had just left Michael, about two years ago, I started working on my third LP which was called *Octopuss*. It wasn't released in America. I think they put one ad in the trades and then it was immediately forgotten."

Over The Top was recorded at both Central Sound Studios in Manchester and Townhouse Studios in London. It was produced by one of Deep Purple's favourite producers, Martin

Birch. It is actually quite frustrating to state that commercially the album was largely overlooked; it's frustrating because musically it features an all-star cast and most importantly, some fantastic tracks. The album includes the small hit single, 'Theme One' by George Martin, which was originally used for BBC Radio One when the network opened in 1967. Don Airey's keyboard playing is phenomenal on Cozy's version of the track, there is even a cheeky quote of the Cream song, 'White Room' (and if it's not actually an intentional quote, then the notes and rhythm used are certainly the same!).

Cozy's drumming on the track also includes a reprise of his rhythm from 'Dance With The Devil'. As much as Cozy seemed to feel that there was more to him as a musician than the very track that made him a household name, it is good to hear him make reference to it in the opening track of his first solo album. The 'Theme One' track has certainly got enough punch to it that it offers something heavier and more along the trademark lines of what Powell was about as a drummer by that time in his career (heavy and known for it, thanks to his work with Rainbow). There are multiple accounts where Cozy advocated that his first solo album was not obstructive or indeed a sore point with Rainbow. Besides, as mentioned in the chapter about Rainbow, it does seem that Cozy was able to assert himself when it was necessary.

The promotional poster for Cozy's *Over The Top* album is frankly brilliant; it plays on the fact that Powell is playing with a cast of brilliant and well known musicians. In huge lettering, it states; "Putting Cozy Powell, Jack Bruce, Don Airey, Dave Clempson, Bernie Marsden, Gary Moore and Max Middleton together in one studio might be called over the top. The album is."

Great advert, says it all really. The fact that the band for the album features so many high-profile musicians is testament to the fact that *Over The Top* is not merely a self-indulgent drum solo frenzy. Far from it; not only does Powell take advantage of the musical talents of the band but he also embraces their talents as songwriters too. The album features jazz rock with the track 'Killer' and yet there is still very much a rock feel to the album overall. Powell jams with an adaptation of the '1812 Overture' on the title track. It's great to hear this on a studio album considering that it was such a prominent feature in many of his live performances, particularly with Rainbow.

Cozy seemed keen to assert that doing a solo album was about real musicianship and wanting to move away from the reputation he perhaps feared he had as a result of the more musically simple singles that he had become well known for commercially. He was quoted in *Sounds* in June 1979; "I started off my career playing with a lot of serious musicians and when I had my solo singles out they were done as a laugh, tongue-in-cheek, you know. I didn't expect them to be successful, but they were and people tend to judge me just on that and forget about the stuff I did eight or nine years ago with the Jeff Back Group. I don't want to be branded that easily, I want to show people that there's more to me than might at first meet the eye. So that's why I did the album. It's not an ego trip, it's something I wanted to do and enjoyed doing."

Over The Top is very much a band album whereby Powell does not make it all about the drums. They drive what the other musicians are doing but it doesn't overshadow them. It is very much to Cozy's credit that the album features the talents of many. It was considered by the reporter in *Melody Maker* in June 1979; "Listening to a couple of tracks provided enough evidence that *Over The Top*, as the album will be titled, is a high quality affair, varied in conception and carefully assembled, and not simply two sides of solid drumming."

The album took just over three weeks to complete. Cozy was quoted in *Melody Maker* in June 1979 as he explained how it wasn't too difficult to get all of the musicians together to make the record; "I just phoned them up and announced that I was doing a solo album this month, and they all agreed to participate — it was as simple as that. I think the last thing Jack Bruce did was *Berlin* for Lou Reed three years ago, and he did something for Zappa two years before that. He's done no work for anybody else recently, just his own albums. I'd always wanted to play with him, because he's a real rock 'n' roll bassist. He came into the studio, played as well as ever, very enthusiastic, and we had a fantastic time."

Tilt was released in 1981 following Powell's departure from Rainbow and having done a brief stint with Graham Bonnet's band. As with *Over The Top*, *Tilt* featured a number of musicians who Cozy had worked with earlier in his career; Jeff Beck, Neil Murray, Bernie Marsden and Frank Aiello.

The album was reviewed in *Cash Box* in December 1981; "This ace drummer has assembled a veritable who's who of fellow Brit rock veterans for *Tilt* and the whole album has a great loose jam feel to it. Switching styles from sax filled blues rock to progressive ELP styled rock to sonic Jeff Beck vamps, Powell changes personnel on almost every song and it comes off showing him as a dynamo among drummers. Gary Moore and Jeff Beck also turn in some spectacular performances on this eclectic mix."

Additionally, *Tilt* includes the talents of some-time King Crimson saxophone player Mel Collins. Inevitably, this makes *Tilt* considerably different to *Over The Top* although once again, Powell made good use of the talents of his fellow musicians on the performing and songwriting front.

The most obvious difference with *Tilt* perhaps is the fact that unlike *Over The Top*, the first side (and only the first side) of the LP contains vocals. Once again, Cozy made an album that is suggestive of the fact that he was a team player. He was quoted in *International Musician and Recording World* in December 1981 "I put a lot of sweat and blood into that album and everyone that is playing on it I'm very proud of."

When asked about the fact that it's not overtly a drummer's album, Cozy replied, "No, I think there are quite enough of them around. People say to me there's not any drum solos on it but drum solos on record, leave it out! Unless it's Buddy Rich where it's something technically fantastic — I don't claim to be Buddy Rich. I prefer to concentrate my energies on doing something where I'm featured with all the people I enjoy working with. The drum sounds on the album took nineteen minutes because I know exactly what I'm doing."

In 1983, Cozy released his third solo album, *Octopuss*. The album features a different line-up once again, including Jon Lord on keyboards. It was in between his work with Robert Plant and Michael Schenker that Cozy managed to squeeze in the time to make *Octopuss*; the album was recorded in just four weeks (that said, by the time *Octopuss* was released, Cozy was with Whitesnake). Cozy used a track by the Philharmonia Orchestra to record the tracks '633 Squadron' and 'The Big Country'. He was quoted on the matter in June 1983 in *Kerrang!*; "I played my drums along to the track they recorded. If I'd played drums with the orchestra, it would have taken a lot longer, and would have cost a fortune. They didn't have that much free time either... I always thought '633 Squadron' would be a good track for a drum solo and I've used that track for a couple of years now, and as for 'The Big Country' — I just love the tune." As with Cozy's first solo album, *Over The Top*, *Octopuss* features a number of jazz and rock numbers.

Octopuss was reviewed by Chris Welch in June 1983 in *Kerrang!*; "Despite all the bombast, the explosive stage spectaculars and the use of what people used to call "commercial" material like big orchestral themes, Cozy remains one of the finest drum technicians in rock, a man who can lay down a violently heavy beat, and throw in some dazzlingly fast licks to boot. And boot he does all the way through this entertaining and highly musical solo album. Cozy's drums are up front most of the way, with a special new recording technique to ensure the bass drums in particular cut through. Be careful they don't shake your speakers to pieces. For those interested in drums for their own sake there is much to be appreciated. Like Cozy's rock steady sense of time, well noted while backing Gary Moore's superb solo on 'Dartmoore' and again on the attractive opening cut 'Up On The Downs'. The pieces range between spectacular showcases for Cozy of the kind he plays nightly on tour with Whitesnake, rockers like 'Formula One' and loose jams like 'Octopuss'. Here Cozy joins forces with bassman Colin Hodgkinson whose doomy grinding bass provides a perfect foil for some drum improvisation. The big epics '633 Squadron' and 'The Big Country' come complete with new orchestral recordings (Cozy used to play along to original versions by Ron Goodwin). Some may call them corny but they certainly give Cozy a chance to play the role of symphonic percussionist, crashing his cymbals and unleashing the famous double bass drums. The cuts are all different, concluding with a superb heavy metal rave up on 'The Rattler' and there is enough guitar work to please even those who still think the drummer should stay in the background."

Great review! It covers the musical diversity that is present on the album whilst addressing (or at least, alluding to) the old debate about whether drummers should be in the background or not. I would advocate that *Octopuss* strongly showcases Cozy not only as a fantastic drummer, particularly in his strong use of bass drums, but as someone who very much had the confidence and professional generosity to share the spotlight with the other musicians.

After *Octopuss*, it was another nine years before Cozy Powell would do another solo album. *The Drums Are Back* was released in 1992. The album was recorded between Powell's two stints with Black Sabbath. After the release of *The Drums Are Back*, Cozy took his band Cozy Powell's Hammer on the road. As with his three earlier solo albums, an all-star cast of musicians feature and there are some excellent tracks on the album.

The EMI Electrola press release for *The Drums Are Back* stated; "The former power drummer with Black Sabbath, Whitesnake and ELP created an absolute classic rock album with a little help from some of the world's best musicians." EMI Electrola pretty much summed it up really. The album has some brilliant highlights including guitar pieces, 'Legend Of The Glass Mountain' and a version of Mason Williams' 'Classical Gas'. Overall, *The Drums Are Back* is a worthwhile album and very much so. It was the last of Cozy Powell's solo albums to be released whilst he was alive. *Especially For You* was released posthumously.

All of Cozy's solo albums are demonstrative of not only his amazing drumming but also the way in which his musicality drove the beauty of the melodies played by other musicians. Powell was the master of using the drum kit to inject further musicality into a beautiful melody. That's something special. He didn't just jam along, he drove the music and punctuated it in ways that arguably, many other drummers may not have done. I'm going to level with you here readers; this chapter is pretty short. I could have gone into great detail about the tracks on each of Cozy's five solo albums but I don't think it would add to the understanding of what Powell's intentions, opinions and ideas may have been whilst working on the albums and sadly, there was not much written about them in the media at the time they were released (or indeed today).

It is sad that the albums didn't get the attention they deserved, at least in the mainstream. In such regard, do listen to them if you have not done so already. They were really undersold at the time but musically, they really do speak for themselves. Go and listen to them and draw your own conclusions. Be sure to make use of the discography in the back of this book. It's a goldmine, I promise.

In particular, Cozy worked with Don Airey on more occasions than is probably widely known; not just in Rainbow and as part of Cozy Powell's Hammer but also on some of Airey's solo projects. For instance, Cozy worked on Don Airey's album, *K2 — Tales Of Triumph And Tragedy*. In a feature on the album in *Music And Media* in November 1988, Airey described the philosophy behind his concept album about the remote Himalayan peak. Airey was quoted; "I am hoping the music will convey the mystery of the place. I have tried to make it symbolic, but people can interpret it in its own way. It started life as an instrumental album, not exactly new age, but then I researched it and met Jim Curran (climber and photographer on the tragic 1986 expedition), I became obsessed and started writing songs for it."

It's a fascinating album both generally and in terms of what it offers as a concept album. As ever, Cozy's drumming certainly adds something and once again, like his time with ELP, the *K2* album shows that Powell's talents were not exclusive to just heavy rock music.

There's loads of Cozy's music that risks getting lost in the whirls of obscurity. Don't let it happen. Probably not many people have heard of Forcefield (perhaps because the band's work was based predominantly on cover songs) but again, that is worth a listen. Sure, the material isn't original but it is certainly reflective of some excellent musicianship. Look at the press release for one of their singles, issued by President Records for the 'Heartache' single on 7th November 1988. It stated; "Forcefield II defy the heavy rock categorisation that seems almost inevitable with a line-up comprised of Ray Fenwick (Ian Gillan Band and Spencer Davis Group),

The Cozy Powell Story

Cozy Powell (Rainbow, Michael Schenker Group, etc.), Jan Akkerman (Focus) and Tony Martin (Black Sabbath). For 'Heartache' is one of several ballads taken from the essentially AOR album entitled *The Talisman*. Jan with clear and concise guitar work joins forces with Tony's sensitive vocals and Ray on second guitar, while Cozy provides the insistent pulse. The song was co-written by Ray together with Pete Prescott, lead vocalist in Forcefield I of 1987. The B-side contains an instrumental version of 'I Lose Again' in which the high calibre of Jan's musicianship is clearly defined." An all-star cast with which Cozy clearly belonged; a little known but worthwhile project indeed.

There are also instances where Cozy had a few near misses with projects that didn't quite get off the ground for any number of reasons, largely perhaps beyond his control. Cozy was quoted in October 1987 in *Rhythm* on a band he was starting with after his time with ELP; "Since the whole ELP fiasco fell apart, I've been doing a lot of session work and one of the things was helping out John Sykes with a project that he's been working on since he left Whitesnake at the beginning of the year. Since the success of their recent album, which John virtually wrote, a lot of record companies have literally been banging on his door. Through that he's got a deal, so we've been working on some bits and pieces for that, with hopefully an album to be recorded by the end of the year. In about three weeks' time I'll know the extent of everything — what the band's going to be called and all that. In fact we're arguing over names at the moment... I sincerely hope this is going to be a contender band — a band that lasts for some time. John, Tony and Ray just want to get on and work hard which is good. It'll be nice to do something positive instead of dilly-dallying around. I love to keep working. It saddens me when a lot of people spend a lot of time discussing it. I'd rather get on and do it. Much more satisfying for the brain.

And because none of the band are superstars, it means they've all got to work hard, which is another good thing. You may notice an air of cynicism creeping in there!"

Disappointingly, the band in question never came to be, at least not with Powell as a member. He was quoted in February 1988 in *Metal Hammer* on the matter; "Well, that's a sad tale. I spent about nine months trying to get that together but because of my contractual situation I couldn't actually sign a deal so John got it himself — and I think he suddenly believed he was the only reason for that deal. He thought Geffen were only interested in him, which may be the case, who knows? But it gave me the impression that I was just "the drummer" of the band (instead of the co-founder). John then appointed his stepfather as manager. I didn't think that was a particularly great idea, and I told him so. It just didn't feel right to me, so rather than commit myself I thought it best to get out then so they could replace me."

How disappointing! Still though, it could be considered that the whole situation was to the benefit of Black Sabbath and indeed to anyone who appreciates how awesome it is that one of the heaviest drummers joined one of the heaviest bands as a result of Powell not having other commitments by the time Tony Iommi wanted Cozy to join his band.

Chapter Twelve:
His Legacy Lives On

Cozy Powell was one of the heaviest rock musicians to get a damn good sound out of a drum kit. He was more than that though. He was versatile yet uncompromising, passionate about his art but not arrogant; keen to bring drumming to the forefront. For every record that Cozy played on that is well known, there is an abundance of them that have sadly faded into obscurity (in such regard, do take a look at the discography at the back of this book).

As well as being an excellent drummer, Cozy was a showman; flames, smoke and explosions augmented phenomenal drum solos onstage. Always exciting. And yet, Cozy was just as proficient in genres outside of the loud and shocking world of rock 'n' roll. Such talent served him well not just when being in ELP but in terms of how capable he was as a session musician; he could get in the studio and deliver what was required of him in very few takes, such was the speed at which 'Dance With The Devil' was made.

As influenced as Cozy was by John Bonham, he still made his drumming very much his own and was unafraid to explore ways in which to do this. Most famously his use of double bass drums was a key element of his technique but equally, his knowledge of recording and production was such that he was often coming up with new ways to get a heavier sound. For instance; how the mics were utilised in the studio for the recording of 'Dance With The Devil' and the way in which the drums were placed in the studio space for the recording of Rainbow's 'Stargazer'.

In many interviews, it comes across that Cozy spoke his mind and yet, not in such a way that came across as unprofessional; a healthy and endearing mixture of honest, diplomatic and candid. It seems that Cozy's approach to dealing with personnel matters in the many bands he was part of was just as professional as the energy and passion that he brought to his drumming.

Equally, he was one of the few drummers to have solo chart success in their own right. It was rare then and it is certainly rare now. It is disappointing that, as much as Cozy advocated against it, drum machines have become so frequently used today and there are so few drummers that now rise to such levels of fame and accomplishment in the public eye compared to what Cozy achieved. He became a household name with 'Dance With The Devil' and as much as the track wasn't perhaps reflective of the music that he truly wanted to make, it was certainly a turning point in his career. Without 'Dance With The Devil', it would perhaps be plausible that Cozy might not have caught the attention of a certain Ritchie Blackmore and then Michael Schenker and so on and so forth.

Of course, Cozy was creative in his own right, building complex and fascinating drum solos around '1812 Overture' and '633 Squadron'. Fittingly, his rolling bass drums sounded like cannon fire.

Cozy Powell was an innovator. He put a lot of well-reasoned thought into how to put both musical and visual excitement into his drumming on stage. He was quoted in *Modern Drummer* about it in November 1984; "I've always had solos in the past, even back to the Jeff Beck days. I want the solo to be something that is very explosive and unforgettable. Although my technical expertise is minimal, I will probably be able to fool most of the people most of the time by what

I do. It's not just a case of playing, it's a case of using every trick in the book. It's possible to play the things you can play with an orchestra, so I use a tape of an orchestra as I play. In Rainbow, I used the '1812 Overture' with the full Minneapolis Symphony Orchestra. I would play to that and there would be a lot of lights and effects. When you saw it, it seemed incredible. It was only me playing a drumkit but when you get a sixty-six-piece orchestra, choir, a few bombs and smoke, it's unforgettable, whether you like drums or not. I've always tried to do a solo that's spectacular. In the Michael Schenker Group, I did a thing where I incorporated the '1812 Overture' and a piece of music from the '633 Squadron', which is a war film about planes bombing Norway, trying to get a nuclear plant the Germans have. It's a very famous piece of music and I would use the theme music in the set because it was very British. I'm now working on a new solo where I'm going to incorporate 'Mars' from *The Planets* suite with a whole bunch of effects, maybe using lasers. It's not very long, maybe eight or nine minutes, but there are great effects. The riser moves and the whole thing. I did that in 1975 with Rainbow and it was the first time anybody actually moved on stage with a drumkit. I had one that went up in the air and out towards the audience. Then everybody started doing that. I got a lot of ideas from Nick Mason, who did a thing with Pink Floyd. He was the first one I ever saw use lights when he played, and I thought it was a very good idea to have strobe lights around the bass drum. It was a very simple effect, but I thought I would expand that. Not everyone in the audience is going to be a drummer so I like to have the element of surprise and do something a bit spectacular."

In the same feature, Powell continued as he advocated for the importance of good showmanship; "When you're playing in a band, the showmanship is always going to come across, but you just hold it back a bit. When you have your chance they say 'take it away', you hit with everything you have, whatever it takes. I'm not saying that I'm trying to disguise my playing and that if I didn't use the effects I couldn't play. I can play but I like to really get it across. The sort of bands I've been playing in, fortunately give me the time and money to spend on all these theatrical effects. It seems to come off. Plus, I enjoy it."

Unlike many of his drumming peers, Cozy Powell was an individual who couldn't settle in one band for too long. Rainbow was the nearest to the exception on the basis that he was with them for five years. That said, whilst Powell made a total of three studio albums with Rainbow, he also did the same with Black Sabbath as well as making five studio albums under his own name and four with Forcefield. All in all, as much as Cozy moved from one band to the other, he was not a job hopper in the derogatory sense of the phrase. He was quoted in *Rhythm* in October 1987; "I must admit that I would have loved to have been in a band that went on for ten years. It's not been my choice to keep moving round, it's just circumstances. Mind you, I was with Rainbow for five years. To last with Ritchie Blackmore that long deserves some sort of endurance medal doesn't it?"

Of course, Powell was probably joking about deserving a medal for working with Ritchie Blackmore for five years. Even where he might have felt frustrated with Rainbow's musical direction which ultimately resulted in him leaving the band in 1980, in the long run, he remained on good terms with Blackmore. In the fanzine, *More Black Than Purple*, Cozy did a very candid interview (such is the relaxed yet informative nature of fanzines) with Jerry Bloom in May 1997. He was quoted; "You'll be pleased to know that Ritchie and I had a very interesting evening's chat yesterday. Very constructive. Very positive. He's probably mellowed a little bit since twenty years ago when we worked together... I haven't seen Ritchie for ten years, maybe more. Ritchie's Ritchie, you take him as he is. I suppose he's just like me, he's a boy who's never grown up and he likes to do stupid things, but I can get along with that, that's fine."

Cozy was also quoted as advocating for the possibility of a reunion of the Blackmore/Dio/Powell line-up of Rainbow; "I think if the situation was right that we got back together for the music side of it, and we were going to do something, I mean just getting involved. I've got mixed feelings. It's always nice, I mean whether I could ever work with Ronnie again, I would have much more of a problem working with him as I find him. He's got very bitter over the last few years. I don't know. I would feel a bit uncomfortable in some respects, although I suppose sometimes professionally you've got to think about what a good thing it would be. I mean if Rainbow got back together again as it was. Say we did a few dates just for the hell of it then I wouldn't say no. I'd be interested. I'd like to work with Ritchie again, because I've thought of a few other things I could do to him which I didn't do in the five years when I worked with him before!"

Powell being professional as ever. On the Ronnie James Dio front, it seems like Cozy was basically saying that even though they didn't get on too well on a personal level, he could put that aside for the sake of the music. I would argue that such a project would have been very much to the credit of both late musicians. Doing such a reunion would have certainly pleased a lot of fans (even today the fan forums can't go a month without someone posting a "no Dio, no Rainbow" type complaint!).

Also in the same interview, Cozy reminisced about the practical jokes he and Blackmore got up to back in the day, including all the Tony Carey stuff (as well as the ones that Cozy and Blackmore had done to each other the very evening of that interview, throwing water from hotel balconies and putting things in each other's hotel rooms to cause annoyance - very immature but happy days I suppose).

In fairness to Powell's legacy, I think it's right that I include the fact that he sounded a fair bit remorseful about what he and Blackmore may have put Carey through back in 1977 when recording *Long Live Rock 'n' Roll* at The Chateau; "It was only sort of after the first tour that the various problems with individual members started coming to the surface. The first person to suffer I think was Tony Carey. The last time I ever saw him he was running down the road with his suitcases in his hands after we'd tried to kill him! I'd forgotten about how funny some of the things were. They obviously weren't very funny to him, but if you think that everybody in the band and crew are all trying to make your life a misery it must have been hell for him. Poor bloke really! We really put that guy through some real shit I have to say. I'd forgotten half of it and Ritchie reminded me last night. 'Don't you remember we did this and don't you remember we did that'."

Cozy recalled the extent of brutality of the pranks played on Tony Carey when asked about a heated doorknob; "It was about two hundred degrees centigrade, so by the time he reached the door... aaagh! And as he pulled the door open there was a plank tied to it, and then he realised we had tried to brick him in! I think he realised that perhaps he wasn't the most popular man in the band at that point. That was just some of the stuff." (that's really not kind is it! In all seriousness it is bullying and it could have seriously compromised Carey's livelihood because you need your hands to be able to play music. However, some people just have a humour for destruction and slapstick and that's just one of those things I suppose).

Finally, Cozy advocated that at the end of the day, there was an element of things being twelve of one and half a dozen of the other; in the Blackmore and Powell vs. Carey situation,

Carey was giving them some attitude anyway; "The problem is that if you're dealing with guys with an English sense of humour, and I guess by that point Ritchie and my sense of humour was pretty warped, and you're starting to come off a bit big time, which he certainly did. We'd say okay Tony, more or less on the second album, would you like to come and do a keyboard solo now? 'Well man I might come down in a couple of hours if I feel like it.' It's like... wrong! You don't do that. When Ritchie says, 'can you come and do a keyboard solo?' you go and do a keyboard solo. So he kind of made a rod for his own back in that respect. He asked for it. He really did. He was a very good player, but very cocky and a bit full of himself. So he had to go. There was no way he was going to last the pace."

Okay, so whilst showing a bit of remorse on the whole Tony Carey situation regarding the crap he and Blackmore put him through, Cozy still seemed to think that the pranks were a little bit justified. Up to him. I'm not the referee here!

The interview occurred on the basis of spontaneity and the fact that Powell was so approachable as a person. The information provided by interviewer, Jerry Bloom, sheds some light on the way in which Powell was happy to be interviewed at the last minute.

It comes across that Powell was gracious, patient and relaxed, as was elaborated on in *More Black Than Purple* in June 1998; "The interview I conducted with Cozy Powell was one of those unforeseen occasions, when the whole thing was utterly spontaneous. I had decided to go to the *Esbjerg Festival* in Denmark when news that Rainbow would headline on the Saturday evening was sprung upon me at short notice. With the possibility that it was going to be Rainbow's only European show for the foreseeable future I booked a flight. As it was, the gig turned out to be Rainbow's last ever concert (as was true at the time of the interview - Blackmore has since gone on tour with a new line-up of Rainbow in recent years). Also on the bill was Peter Green's Splinter Group, which at the time included Neil Murray and of course Cozy Powell. Flying out the day before the gig I happened to be on the same plane as Peter Green's entourage. At the check-in desk I recognised a couple of the band, and it instantly occurred to me that Cozy would be around somewhere. I'd never met him but as the legendary drummer had been such a major part of early Rainbow, the possibility of having a quick chat with him at the airport soon dawned on me… He immediately struck me as a very approachable guy."

Before he had even boarded the flight, Powell was happy to commit to doing an interview later that weekend. He wasn't fazed by the interviewer turning up much later than scheduled. It was advocated of Cozy's demeanour; "He came across as a very honest, sincere and regular guy. There was none of the "Rock Star" bullshit that accompanies some people. There was nothing pretentious about him and no heirs and graces."

The interview took place less than a year before Cozy's untimely death. It's good to know through this interview that Powell and Blackmore remained friends in the long run and that even though Powell and Dio didn't particularly get on personally, it was not to the extent that the door had been closed on the possibility of a reunion as fellow musicians.

Powell's honesty and no bullshit approach to the music business was arguably an endearing quality about him. His cynicism was probably justified based on a whole plethora of experiences. He was quoted in *Rhythm* in October 1987; "The trouble is that this is the music business and a lot of things have happened over the years — broken promises, people not telling you what's going on — so I'm not counting on anything until I'm sitting behind the kit on stage and we're off."

Fair enough, we are all a product of our environment. Powell was quoted in *Modern Drummer* in November 1984;

"I'm cynical about this business. I love playing music and I think that music and the business have somehow become entwined. I don't like many people in the business. That's nothing personal there, but I don't like most record company executives, most reporters and most other musicians. That's kind of a sweeping statement isn't it? And people are asking 'who does he think he is?' But I've been around for a long time, I've seen a lot of people come and go and I don't like what I've seen most of the time. The people I've known for years and years are fine and there are a lot of people coming up who are great. There are also a lot of jerks in this business. People latch onto musicians in bands because it's "in" this week. I think you really have to take care of yourself in this business. My idea of relaxing, if I can use the term, is going back to my farm on my own with my animals. They don't answer back, they're just there and that's great. I can just wander about, see the fields and do things I wouldn't dream of when I'm on the road, because all I see on the road is hotel rooms, debauchery, airports and the gigs. It's just one long continual chaos. I don't care what people say, it is that. There's no doubt about it. You look at it and think 'what am I doing here?' You go home to a farm and it's so opposite. The farmer next door to me has never been further than twenty miles. He's never been to London for example. He's out in the fields everyday, he's been there for sixty years, he rarely has a drink and I come back and see him and think 'if only he knew what I've been up to the last six months', that to me is so completely different from a tour, and that's what it's all about for me. I've spent all my money on getting that place and it'll take me a long time to pay it off but that's why I do it. Everybody needs a release and some time to unwind. That's why I live there. I love London and I love big cities, but sometimes I have to get away to recharge."

Never a truer word spoken there Cozy! I think we can all relate to that no matter what walk of life we're from; the search for a bit of peace and quiet amongst all of life's noise (and not just the musical kind!).

In the same feature, Cozy was quoted; "I've been through most of the things you go through. Most of the bands who are superstars haven't been playing for all that long or haven't had success for that long. I haven't had superstar status, but I've been in enough groups that have been popular. Jeff Beck was the most popular band I was with in the States so the first tour of America I did was with Jeff. I was thrown into a situation with that kind of adulation and I've never been in that type of situation again. Most of the people I know in the business who have been through it for a long time are nice people. You couldn't wish for a nicer man than Jon Lord. He's an absolute gentleman. People who have been around for a long time haven't any need to show off anymore. Maybe, as you get older, you suddenly realise there is no point in showing off. I'm sure most kids, if they do go through a phase like that, will come out of it and realise they've been a bit of an idiot. Then they'll calm down."

It seems like despite all of the noise and turbulence of the rock 'n' roll lifestyle that surrounded Cozy throughout his musical career, he wasn't so engulfed in it that it was to his detriment. In numerous interviews he advocated for keeping healthy in order to be able to play well. It really comes across that he was in it for the music rather than the fame and/or the associated messing about that probably comes with that.

It could easily be advocated that Powell was his own person who appreciated his own space and his life outside of the music business. He was quoted in *Kerrang!* in July 1986; "Having this place keeps me sane. I don't farm myself, although the house is literally a farmhouse. I have got horses here in the stables, but no cattle. I come from Cirencester originally which is an agricultural town. Sometimes if I'm feeling energetic I go and help the local farmer get the hay in! It's all a far cry from some of the seedier places in the world of rock 'n' roll that I've played in. It makes a pleasant change to arrive here. It's the only thing that keeps me going. When people ask how I still manage to play with the same enthusiasm, I think it's because I've got this place. It's so relaxing. It brings you down to earth. You can't get away with being a superstar down here. Not that I do that anyway, but if I tried they'd just take the mickey. Everyone's on the same footing 'round here. I don't go hobnobbing with Rod Stewart in the night clubs; why go out when you've got a nice peaceful place like this? I'm on the road for eight months of the year and when I come home I want to relax."

An Englishman's home is his castle and all that. Not in the literal Ritchie Blackmore sense of the phrase, but still.

It really comes across that Powell was about the music and not the politics and stuff that probably came with it. Sure, he was involved with it all but as much as he wanted to bring drumming to the forefront, he seemed to take an active interest in wanting the music to be good as a whole.

He was quoted in *Rhythm* in October 1987 in a way that really seemed to convey him as caring about good music as an overall thing and it not just being all about him and his music; "There's a shortage of really classy English hard rock bands at the moment. The Americans seem to be taking over. But the fact that Whitesnake went to number two in America the other week shows there must still be a market for that sort of thing. Rock 'n' roll touring is not much fun these days, especially when you're coming in with a band that is virtually starting again. It's a lot of schlepping about, doing one or two years of supporting people who give you all kinds of grief, coaches round America, lots of driving, no time to do anything else. I wouldn't exactly call that fun. Yet it's also very satisfying and gives you the opportunity to play every day. And if you're good and the band's good, the rewards will come later. When you can headline and do a good show which people will talk about for years for come. I'm a great believer in entertaining the public and giving them a larger than life show. I have to say though, that the business hassles have almost got to the point where I've given up. I'm not a fan of the business. I don't want to be pictured with a star from *Eastenders*. And I've noticed there's not so much fun in the business as there used to be. Perhaps that's just me being cynical. If you think of the American scene — Journey, Heart — the beat is simple but very heavy. The material dictates it that way, and also since the disco explosion and that thump, thump, thump; everybody's been brainwashed into accepting doing it by the book. When I think back to what I was playing in the seventies with Rainbow, there were a whole load of rhythms there. It was much more exciting. Yet the Whitesnake stuff later on was really simple. I almost let myself down there. Now we have a load of extremely clinical players. Where have all the great drummers gone? Keith Moon? Mitch Mitchell? The business needs some outlandish characters to come back and excite it all up again. There's a great gap of good hard rock bands too. Free, Bad Company, Deep Purple, Led Zeppelin, Jethro Tull — those bands have fizzled out or made their reappearance in a diluted form."

Anyone who cares about music more than their own ego and playing the whole fame game has arguably got to be someone worth listening to. I advocate strongly that Powell could definitely be placed in such category.

It is amazing to consider that if Cozy Powell had stuck with just one band, or maybe even just two or three at the very most, his musical legacy would not be as expansive as it is. I think that for anyone who enjoys good drumming and indeed good music, the fact that Powell played in so many bands is advantageous in terms of the breadth of discography that exists as a result. It is perhaps in such regard that Cozy's enthusiasm for bringing the drums into further recognition by the public was better facilitated as in, if you heard Cozy's drumming through just one of the bands he was in, it is possible that you would want to hear the music of other projects that he was involved with. It was a phenomenal achievement on Cozy's part really as in, how many drummers, who have been musically active in recent years, can be easily recognised as household names. It was rare for drummers to have solo singles and albums at the time Cozy Powell did it and it is still a rare occurrence today. It is still rare for a drummer to be recognised as such in their own right. Not only this, but when Cozy was with a band, he was more than just the drummer. With Black Sabbath, he was involved in the production process and with Rainbow, he was innovative in how to get the best sound out of the space available in the recording environment.

Powell didn't just play drums. He did more than that, not just musically but executively. He was quoted in *Sounds* in June 1979 regarding his contribution to helping Ritchie Blackmore recruit new talent to the band; "Ritchie brought Roger Glover in as the producer of the new album. Meanwhile we were trying to find a bass player, keyboard player and singer. So I said, 'okay Ritchie, let's stop messing around, let's get a good keyboard player in. I know someone, he used to be in my band Hammer. He's great, he's a good writer, a nice guy, no problems.' So Don Airey joined the band."

Cozy was also proactive in the process of trying to find a new bass player for Rainbow. Although his suggestions weren't what the band ultimately went with, it was still demonstrative of the extent to which Powell was a proactive member of Rainbow beyond being a drummer; "The bass player was a little more tricky. I got Clive Chaman in from the Jeff Beck Group, he also used to be a member of Hammer. However he didn't really work out. He's a funky sort of player, he needs a lot of freedom and he wouldn't have got that with Ritchie.

After a while we were going crazy, we couldn't find anybody at all. Then Roger Glover (who had already been recruited to the band as a producer) said, 'Well, what about me?' Ritchie asked me what I thought as I'd have to work with the guy and I said, 'fair enough, I'll give it a try, once I start playing I can never hear anybody else anyway', so Roger became the bass player."

And finally, Powell was enthusiastic about the recruitment of Graham Bonnet to the band, which would complete the new line-up of Rainbow for their 1979 album, *Down To Earth*; "He's (Bonnet) got a four-octave range, which is what we want. He's a very, very good singer. He came out to the Chateau in Geneva where we were recording, sang over some backing tracks we'd laid down and — boom! — he hit it straight off, he was great. We were all biting our lips, trying not to smile... he'd really got it down well. So he's now in the band."

Powell was quoted in *Modern Drummer* in November 1984; "I've enjoyed working in all the bands I've worked with. People say that I move around a lot but I've only moved because the situations I've been in have gone over the top for some reason or another."

Evidently and particularly in the context of Rainbow, his most long-term engagement, Powell was not a fence sitter. He took an active role in the band and seemed to be passionate about getting involved with the things that mattered. It wasn't just about the drumming. There are plenty of drummers who I'm sure would be more passive about the whole thing. At the beginning of the *Down To Earth* era line-up of Rainbow, Cozy seemed very enthusiastic about the band, as he was quoted in *Sounds* in June 1979; "This is a very strong line-up, possibly the strongest Rainbow have ever had. All the members we've got are very competent at what they do. Don's been playing keyboards for years, Roger's an accomplished bass player and

Graham's a great singer."

Even though Rainbow was (and still is) Ritchie Blackmore's band, Powell took an extent of interest in it to the point that he cared about the direction the band was taking. It went beyond just turning up and drumming. Powell was further quoted in the same edition of *Sounds;* "To my mind Rainbow is a very heavy rock band, there should be no compromises. Ritchie feels that we should compromise to a certain extent and therefore this album has a couple of commercial numbers on it. Of course there's the usual heavy stuff as well, but like I say it does contain these two commercial tracks. Ritchie and I have argued about their inclusion, well we have a lot of arguments anyway as you can well imagine. When we don't agree over certain things he usually wins because it's his band, he started it all in the first place, so I'm not going to knock that. But I will make my opinions heard. I'll say what I think to Ritchie and he respects me for it. I think the only reason that I'm still a member of Rainbow is that Ritchie knows that I'll beat him up if he fires me. So we have differences of opinion — in fact it nearly came to fisticuffs at one point in Geneva — but at the end of the day it's usually okay, we have a few drinks and make it up. But it's good all the same, it's healthy. We're men enough to know that united we stand, divided we don't necessarily fall but it's not going to be so easy. So if we stick together we could end up conquering the world. Which'd be nice, wouldn't it?"

Damn! Thinking about those comments of Cozy's makes me (and probably loads of other fans!) really wish that Rainbow had managed to sort at least one kind of reunion with Cozy Powell in the line-up, he was clearly a very important element to the musical and personnel chemistry of that band.

Cozy was quoted in *Rhythm* in October 1987 as he explained with candour about how long he typically stayed with a band for; "Two years seems to be about my limit, it's true. But although people have given me a lot of criticism for it in the past, I don't actually join bands in order to leave within the year. It's just that circumstances dictate it. Anybody who knows me well will know that I'm not an unreasonable person to work with... it's just that when it comes to telling people what I think, I'm just a bit unsubtle, a bit too blatant. I like to think of myself as pretty down to earth. I can't stand people who think they are God's gift. I won't pander to their whims and emotions. The trouble is that in this business, people do like to have their egos flattered and if you tell them they sang or played something badly, they just don't like it. If somebody doesn't like what I do and they say it to me, fair enough, but when the position is reversed and I tell them, harsh words follow and before you know it, you're out of a job or you've left the job. It always seems to happen, but then I always say at least you know where you stand with me!"

Powell's honesty and sense of ownership of the music was probably to his credit. In the same interview he was quoted; "Drummers are supposed to sit back, play when they're told to play, but otherwise shut up. Band leaders have always got a funny rapport with drummers, mainly because they tend to underestimate them. When I think of it though, the drummer friends of mine who have made a reasonable success of their careers have always said their piece and been very instrumental in the success of the band."

Passion for drumming and self-belief in what he was doing; two qualities that were arguably key drivers behind what made Cozy Powell the success that he was. Although his drumming technique wasn't necessary orthodox, it was always inspired and he went to auditions with a balls-to-the-wall sort of attitude that served him well.

He was quoted in October 1987 in *Rhythm*; "I've always been expressive in my playing. I don't know whether you've seen the Kodo drummers, but I saw a film of them when I was very young and it stuck in my mind. I do think there's a lot of technique in the people who can sit there and play these most intricate rhythms very quietly, but I like to hit things and hit them hard. It's become ingrained in my style of playing. Not very subtle, true, but it hasn't done me much harm in the past. That's exactly why I got the job with Jeff Beck — which in those days was more jazz-rock, and that's exactly why I got the job with Rainbow. I remember the audition for Blackmore. He'd gone through I don't know how many drummers before I came along, I think it was getting into three figures! I knew he was desperate when he tried to persuade me to come out of retirement from motor racing. I mean, he had an idea I might be right, but he wasn't sure because he hadn't seen me play for years. I went over and I thought, well if I'm going to go into this, I might as well do it properly. I psyched myself up, went into the room and said 'right, where's the kit, what are we going to do?' he said, 'let's do a shuffle', so I went bang! And played this shuffle for ten minutes flat out. His fingers were going up and down the fret board and it was like oh my goodness me! because all the other drummers had been sitting there afraid to play. I got the job with Jeff Beck in a similar situation. I took my old Ludwig kit along and set it up right in front of him and flailed away like a complete lunatic. I thought, well if I don't get the job, at least he'll never forget me! My advice to anyone is to play your heart out, at least you'll get noticed if nothing else!"

In all honesty there isn't that much known about Cozy Powell in terms of his personal life. Compared to lots of other musicians and indeed drummers in the public eye at the same time, little is known about his home life, family life, social life etc etc. But here's the thing; whilst I could have gone down the route of trying to source more information from the people who knew Cozy, I don't feel that such approach would have been appropriate on the basis that if Powell chose for things not to be in the public domain when he was alive then who am I to go digging for further information that isn't really mine to give. I'm a massive believer in maintaining a person's legacy in a way that they may have preferred and I tremendously hope that I have managed to achieve that in writing this book.

Besides, there is so much to say about Cozy's music and the antics and strategies he embraced whilst working with so many weird and wonderful people throughout his career. I figure that collating information that was already out there was the best way to tell Cozy's story in a way that maintains the dignity and indeed fascination of his legacy. What matters is that Cozy Powell's contribution to drumming and rock music as a whole was phenomenal and inspirational. Like Ginger Baker in the 1960s, in the 1970s, Cozy Powell was the drummer who needed to be seen to be believed and that was certainly the case when it came to his showmanship and the use of special effects like those used in his '1812 Overture' solos.

There are so many projects that Cozy Powell was active on that many of them have not been well documented. This is due to a combination of some projects being very small scale on a commercial basis but also due to the fact that session musicians were not always credited for their work as such. As a result of this, it is plausible that Cozy Powell's discography could be far greater than that which is documented in this book or indeed, anywhere else. It would certainly be fascinating if years from now, more information came to light on the matter. I'm not sure that it would but we can certainly hope so. I genuinely believe it to be the case that everything listed in the discography of this book is well worth a listen, both in and of itself and in terms of it being demonstrative of Cozy Powell as a drummer.

Cozy was quoted in *Sounds* in March 1978; "I've played on literally hundreds of albums and singles, but I don't get the time anymore 'cos Rainbow is such a full-time job. It's a bit of a shame in many ways as you get no chance for real expansion in a band like Rainbow. It's a rock 'n' roll band. No more, no less, that's all. Nothing jazzy or anything. Sometimes it's nice to play with a variety of people so you get the chance to play some other kind of music. I enjoy recording. It's painless to me. If I don't get a backing track down in two or three takes, I leave it 'till the next day. If it takes you fifteen takes, you have no energy, you get bored with the track. It's pretty easy for the drummer anyway, you just bung it down, and if it's got the feel, you leave it. Then you come back a week later and listen to what's been put on top, the guitars, vocals, keys, and that's when it gets exciting. There are some great songs that work so well in the studio but somehow don't work in front of a live crowd, but that's a whole other story. I think bands that use tapes are a cop out. They may as well not go on the road. I'll go back to session work if I ever get sick and tired of playing on the road."

That's what I mean when I say that the discography that most people state as being Cozy Powell's full discography is quite possibly just the tip of the iceberg. There are lots of sources that estimate Cozy's total participation on albums and singles to be at around sixty something (probably because with the Internet, estimations can often be accepted as fact if they're communicated repeatedly enough across a range of unofficial sources).

Cozy was quoted as having said that he'd played on hundreds of albums and singles. I'm happy to take that as fact, especially when you take into account that during his days with RAK, it was pretty common for session musicians not to be credited, especially because many of them had yet to become famous and thus marketable as such. The same applies with the recordings that Cozy Powell made at the very start of his career. I can say with certainty that there exists

45rpm singles by The Sorcerers and by Young Blood (who were signed to Pye Records), all of which are considerably rare and valuable. But when it comes to details about Cozy's early career, not enough is known. It is absolutely plausible that other recordings exist under all kinds of band names. There is still more research to be done on the matter on a wider scale. Trippy really when you think about it.

Throughout his drumming career, it comes across that Cozy was very consistent as a team player in how he had a good understanding of what the other musicians he was working with needed. He recognised the individual nature of their creative processes and it is very plausible that such approach made him a good person to work with. He was quoted on this in *Rhythm* in October 1987; "Ritchie Blackmore will wring it out as though it's some kind of torture, as though it's agony to get a riff out of his guitar. You know, shaking his head, 'No, no, don't like that', and you'll be playing all the time while he tries to get it right. Of course, when he does it's stunning, but in the meantime it's hard work. Keith Emerson, he'll hear the rhythm in his head exactly and he'll write it out for you or program the drum machine (and say) 'this is what I want you to play', any variation on that and he's not really too happy. I suppose you could say his approach is academic rock. Everybody's got their own little way of doing things and you've got to be prepared to move with their whims. You don't want to bludgeon your way through and play what you want to play. I've known a few drummers put themselves out of a job that way. Maybe once you have got it down you can start throwing in your little extras — a hi-hat bit here, a little cymbal crash there, a tom break and so on. But you can always learn more from what other people's thoughts are on what you should be doing. You can learn what works and what doesn't and what sounds dreadful! But the great thing about being a drummer is that providing you don't become too tied down to one particular style, then you can work with just about anyone... I usually try to adapt my style to the band. I try to bring at least fifty percent or more likely seventy-five percent of me into the band and then adapt that to the music. I think it's important to make your mark. But obviously, the person writing the material has got their idea of which way they think the material's going to go so it's no good blasting your way through it like a sledgehammer."

In the same feature, Cozy was quoted on what it was like to work with Stevie Wonder; "Stevie Wonder is one of these men who walks round singing all day, tapping out rhythms. The man is music. When I worked with him — which was very briefly — he'd come in with this idea in his head and he'd say 'hey, play this man', and he'd start tapping something out on the table. You'd watch and start tapping along with him and he'd get all excited and say 'Yeah, yeah, yeah, now try this in the hi-hat man, try this...' After five minutes you'd have come up with something, and then perhaps you'd do a little bit more or a little bit less of it, and if he really liked it he'd start dancing around and laughing and waving his arms about. Then he'd leap on the keyboards and start playing. It was all very energetic, good stuff and really easy to do. You weren't aware it was work."

Hang on a minute? Cozy Powell worked with Stevie Wonder? Yep, he sure did! However, there may not be recorded material of this available on official release. Cozy himself wasn't even sure on the matter. He was quoted regarding it in *Modern Drummer* in November 1984 when asked about whether he is on the official release of the famous Stevie Wonder song, 'Superstition'; "I don't know. There were so many versions done that I don't even know to this day whether that's me playing. Stevie used to nick bits here and there. You'd do a track and you'd find the next day that the cymbals were taken off and something else was put on. All

I know is that I played on it the very first time he put it down.
I remember the sessions well though. I think we cut two or
three tracks, of which 'Superstition' was one. Jeff (Beck) did
a couple of bits and pieces on his album at the time. There was
this big argument in the control room and Jeff said, 'that's it!'
We flew back to London on a Saturday and Monday morning
a letter came through the post stating 'you are no longer
required' from Jeff's manager who was also a solicitor. I've
forgiven Jeff since for that. In fact, I was with him just last
night."

This is what I mean when I say that it is possible that the
full extent of Cozy Powell's discography will never be known.
If the man himself wasn't sure, then what chance does anyone
else have of being able to compile a definitive list? It's a bit
frustrating really but equally it is symptomatic of, and indeed
an insight into, what the music industry was like when Cozy
was active in it as both a session musician and band member.

Powell was quoted in *Modern Drummer* in November
1984; "Some of the stuff I did I didn't even remember until I
heard it on the radio. It's really strange."

Cozy's passing was announced in April 1998 in *Billboard*
with much taste. There were all manner of gory details
documented in the British press. I'm not going to elaborate
on them because a) they are easily accessible if you want to
read them and b) there is so much more to Cozy Powell's
legacy than the tragic details surrounding how he died. It is
for those very reasons that I am going to share with you (what
I consider to be) one of the more dignified reports on Cozy's
passing; "Colin "Cozy" Powell died April 5 in a car crash near
Bristol in southeast England. He was fifty. Powell, a noted
session drummer who emerged from the sixties beat scene,
came to greater attention in 1971 with the Jeff Beck Group.
He enjoyed solo chart success in the UK with the top twenty
singles, 'Dance With The Devil' (1973), 'The Man In Black'

(1974), and 'Na Na Na' (1974), all produced by Mickie Most and released on the latter's RAK label. 'The Man In Black' was also a Billboard hot one hundred in 1974. The following year, Powell joined ex-Deep Purple guitarist, Ritchie Blackmore in Rainbow, leaving in 1980 and subsequently playing with Michael Schenker, Whitesnake, Emerson, Lake and Powell and Black Sabbath. More recently, he had been recording and playing with Fleetwood Mac founder Peter Green (in Splinter Group), Brian May and Yngwie Malmsteen. Powell was mixing a new solo album before his death. He leaves no next of kin."

What a legacy! What an adventure! There was so much more to Cozy Powell than his more famous works and in particular, 'Dance With The Devil'. He was a talented musician who achieved a lot in a career that spanned decades.

A private funeral service was held at an undisclosed location, it was followed by a memorial service. Further down the line, as was reported in January 2016 in *Classic Rock;* "A memorial plaque in honour of the late drummer Cozy Powell is to be unveiled in his hometown of Cirencester. The tribute comes after fans petitioned town councillors to pay tribute to his career." The event was held on 7th January 2016 at 2.30pm at the Corn Hall, Market Place in Cirencester.

I hope that in writing this book, I have done justice to Cozy Powell's legacy and communicated his story in a way that is informative and authentic. This book contains a mixture of opinions as well as a range of facts that stand up in their own right. Equally though, as my telling of the Cozy Powell story draws to a close, I think it's ultra-important that the last words in the story are told by the people who knew Cozy Powell best from having had the pleasure of knowing and working with him. Many people who knew Cozy have a lot of very positive, kind and endearing things to say about him. It is with all the love in the world that I shall leave you with the following quotes, sadly including some from fellow musicians who have also since passed on...

"We first met nearly thirty years ago and I've known him all his career. We had some great times together. He was certainly hot-headed. He liked driving fast, and jokes and pranks. He's always been a little bit prone to accidents — he swerved one time to miss a deer and he turned the car over. He had accidents, but always came out okay."

"He was one of my dearest friends. We had many great times together. I will miss him greatly. My heart goes out to his family and all his friends. It is a very sad time. Goodbye to one of the greatest rock drummers of all time and a wonderful, caring human being. Your legend will live on! RIP Cozy. Love ya mate!"
Tony Iommi

"His death has been a great shock. He will always remain with us; his friendship always valued, and his music immortalised."
Ritchie Blackmore

"Cozy was a great drummer and a great guy, and he had his own sound."
Bobby Rondinelli

"Cozy Powell was a classic rocker. The best there was."
Roger Daltrey

"We go back years to the days he played with Jeff Beck. Cozy was a great drummer and a great guy."
Carmine Appice

"Cozy was a meaningful and supportive man in my life. Over the past few years he had suffered a number of accidents and my care for him, and concerns were expressed to him... Cozy, in my opinion was one of the greatest hard rock drummers in history, a direct speaking man with a love for many things, including his deep love for fast cars. I believe he'll be missed by many, many people. The legend will go on. Cozy will remain in my heart until I die. The last time we saw each other, we hugged and held onto each other tightly, two old rockers in the spirit of friends and drummers alike, each respecting the other. God bless you Coze, you crazy so and so. I will miss you Coze. I won't forget you or what you've shared with me. I am better for knowing you. Thank you."

Bill Ward

"The musical world has lost a legend and I've lost a friend in the passing of Cozy Powell. His brilliance as a drummer was evident to everyone who heard him perform but it will always be his irrepressible spirit and full appetite for life that those fortunate enough to have known him intimately will remember. Cozy's physical presence may have gone but his place in our hearts will never be forgotten."

Ronnie James Dio

"He was a great character, marvellous musician and a good friend to us both and our family. It was a privilege to have known him and to have worked with him so often over the last twenty-five years. RIP Cozy — we will always miss you and be thinking of you."

Don and Doris Airey

"The world has lost a great man. Cozy Powell was one of those larger than life characters that one meets very rarely in life. Although we hadn't seen much of each other in the last few years, we were still firm friends. The first time I met him was in Musicland Studios in Munich where he had just finished working on *Rainbow Rising*. I played him some of my solo album, *Elements* and he was so encouraging and enthusiastic I gave him a credit on the album. The last time I saw him was during the *Purpendicular* tour in England — he had come by to say hello and wish us well on our new venture. I am devastated by the news of his death. His challenging, lop sided grin and easy-going charm endeared him to everyone and anyone fortunate enough to meet him. During my time in Rainbow we shared many a laugh and many adventures — stories about him are legion. He did nothing in half measures and the title of one of his solo albums was appropriate, *Over The Top*. He was an extraordinary man. My thoughts and condolences go out to those who were closest to him, his family and loved ones. We will mourn him but they will miss him the most. Cozy Powell RIP."

Roger Glover

"I have so many memories of living and working with Cozy. Those daft days in the Midlands, the house in Rectory Road, The Bell pub in Whittington village. I can remember our last chat on the phone when we talked about Bedlam and how by a strange coincidence, the band was linked together by phone calls from around the world last time I visited Frank (Aiello). My heart goes out to dear Frank, who was always there for Cozy and who is now missing his best friend."

Denny Ball

"I shall miss Cozy's sense of humour, his warmth, and his support. He had abundance of natural talent, but above all he was one of the most down to earth people I've ever known. I'll never really be able to accept that he's no longer around."

Glenn Tipton

"He knew and respected his limitations and when he surpassed himself, which was often, there was never a boastful laugh. Everything he did was omni-directional, he was a great guy that nobody knew from whence he came. It is even sadder that Cozy didn't know where he came from either. While bearing a wonderful sense of humility, he'd be pushing the envelope, knowing when to lick it down and post it. He was a fun time enigma unto himself. A revered enigma by all of the people he worked with. Above all, one hell of a great drummer... Somewhere I have some Super 8 footage of Emerson, Lake and Powell on board an aeroplane to their next gig. Cozy is acting the clown demonstrating the oxygen mask routine over the flight attendants drill. We're all laughing. Cozy is using a plastic cup for the oxygen mask and getting entangled in his belt at the same time. Hilarious! I miss you man!"

Keith Emerson

"Cozy was a close friend. He was bright, witty and very warm. In addition, he was a great musician. His loss will be felt by all those who knew him or worked with him." *Greg Lake*

"He didn't suffer fools at all! The ultimate professional and a star above everyone else. He was a hero, and I'd known him twelve years. I can't tell you how sad I was when he died. I loved him to bits, and there's a great void now. But I always imagined he'd go out that way. I never pictured him as an old man with a walking stick. If he'd have got that far I'm sure he'd have topped himself! He'd have driven over a cliff! 'Fuck this! I'm going!'"

Tony Martin

"Cozy was always full of liveliness, energy and enthusiasm. He was a mix of different personalities, but the main thing is, he was a livewire, always putting as much as he could into something — being very professional and wanting everyone to play to the top of their form. He didn't like it if someone wasn't giving as much as he was — if someone was slacking, look out!" *Neil Murray*

"Legendary, and a charismatic star, a lovely bloke."
  Darren Wharton

"I am deeply saddened by the death of Cozy Powell who was a friend, collaborator and mentor. His spirit will live on forever through all the fans he touched during his life and his fantastic music that will always be with us."
  Yngwie Malmsteen

"Drummed for me on several early albums, the best being *Rough And Ready*, here you can witness original and unique cymbal finesse, not to mention powerful playing, as he will be best remembered for."
  Jeff Beck

On his Youtube channel on 6th April 2018, Brian May posted a video statement in memory of Cozy (5th April 2018 marked twenty years since Cozy's tragic passing). In the video, May said; "What a wonderful thing to do to get together to commemorate Cozy. It's twenty years down the line, I can hardly believe it you know... What can I say except I miss him as a brother. We had such an amazing time together and Cozy really gave me the confidence to step outside of Queen and to do things on my own and with somebody who had great sympathy for where I was at, and I felt that I had great sympathy for where he was at... We brought our respective sounds together and boy, we had some fun. It was just amazing. In the studio first of all, then we did a couple of great tours together. Unbelievable! I always felt grateful that Cozy kind of endorsed the hidden things inside me and I hope I did the same for him. I just wanna say that I'm with you all and I loved Cozy and I still do and I always will. And thank you for keeping his memory alive, thank you for keeping his music alive. I'm gonna go home tonight and just play all the stuff he did. And all the great things, including 'Since You Been Gone'… what a wonderful epitaph that is really, for Cozy. God bless him. Let's all remember him, always this way, for the great guy he was."

Appendices

BANDS

The Sorcerers (1967–1968)
Young Blood (1968–1969)
The Ace Kefford Stand (1969)
Big Bertha (1969–1970)
The Jeff Beck Group (1970–1972)
Bedlam (1972–1973)
Cozy Powell (1973–1974, 1979 — 1983, 1992)
Cozy Powell's Hammer (1974, 1992 — 1993)
Rainbow (1975–1980)
Graham Bonnet (1980–1981)
Michael Schenker Group (1980–1982)
Whitesnake (1982–1985)
Emerson, Lake & Powell (1985–1986)
Pete York/Cozy Powell (1987)
Black Sabbath (1988–1991, 1994–1995)
The Brian May Band (1991–1992, 1993 — 1994, 1998)
Peter Green Splinter Group (1997 — 1998)
Tipton, Entwistle and Powell (1997)
Yngwie Malmsteen (1997)
The Snakes (1998)

BAND PERSONNEL

Jeff Beck Group
Jeff Beck – guitars, bass guitar and production
Bobby Tench – vocals and rhythm guitar
Max Middleton – piano and keyboards
Clive Chaman – bass guitar
Cozy Powell – drums

Bedlam
Dave Ball – guitar
Denny Ball – bass
Frank Aiello – vocals
Cozy Powell – drums

Rainbow
Ronnie James Dio – vocals
Ritchie Blackmore – guitar
Tony Carey – keyboards
Jimmy Bain – bass
Cozy Powell – drums

Ronnie James Dio – vocals
Ritchie Blackmore – guitars
Bob Daisley – bass
David Stone – keyboards
Tony Carey – keyboards
Cozy Powell – drums

Ritchie Blackmore – guitar
Graham Bonnet – vocals
Don Airey – keyboards
Roger Glover – bass guitar
Cozy Powell – drums

Michael Schenker Group
Gary Barden – vocals
Michael Schenker – lead guitar
Paul Raymond – keyboards, rhythm guitar
Chris Glen – bass
Cozy Powell – drums

Whitesnake
David Coverdale – lead vocals
Mel Galley – guitars, backing vocals
Micky Moody – guitars
Colin Hodgkinson – bass
Jon Lord – keyboards
Cozy Powell – drums

Appendices

David Coverdale – lead vocals
Mel Galley – guitars, backing vocals
John Sykes – guitars
Neil Murray – bass
Jon Lord – keyboards
Cozy Powell – drums

Emerson, Lake and Powell
Keith Emerson – keyboards
Greg Lake – vocals, guitars, bass
Cozy Powell – drums

Forcefield
Ray Fenwick – guitars, keyboards
Pete Prescott – lead vocals
Mo Foster – bass
Neil Murray – bass
Chris Cozens - keyboards
Nick Magnus – keyboards
Barry St. John – backing vocals
Cozy Powell – drums

Tony Martin – lead and backing vocals
Neil Murray – bass
Ray Fenwick – guitars
Jan Akkerman – electric and acoustic guitars
Lawrence Cottle – bass
Chris Cozens – keyboards
Barry St. John – backing vocals
Cozy Powell – drums

Jan Akkerman – guitars
Ray Fenwick – guitars
Chris Cozens – keyboards
Terry Pack – bass
Mo Foster – bass
Johnny Mars – harmonica
Graham Bonnet – vocals
Cozy Powell – drums

Graham Bonnet – vocals
Ray Fenwick – guitars, keyboards
Bernie Marsden – guitars
Micky Moody – guitars
Mario Parga – guitars
Don Airey – keyboards
Tim Hinkley – organ, keyboards
Terry Pack – bass
Chris Cozens – keyboards
Barry St. John – backing vocals
Cozy Powell – drums

Black Sabbath
Tony Iommi – guitars, producer
Geoff Nicholls – keyboards
Tony Martin – lead vocals
Laurence Cottle – bass
Cozy Powell – drums, producer
Tony Iommi –guitars, production
Tony Martin – lead & backing vocals
Neil Murray – bass
Geoff Nicholls – keyboards
Cozy Powell – drums, production

Tony Iommi – guitars
Tony Martin – vocals
Neil Murray – bass
Geoff Nicholls – keyboards
Cozy Powell – drums

The Brian May Band
Brian May – guitar and vocals
Mike Caswell — guitar
Spike Edney — keyboards
Neil Murray — bass
Maggie Ryder – backing vocals
Miriam Stockley – backing vocals
Chris Thompson – backing vocals
Cozy Powell — drums

Brian May – guitar and vocals
Jamie Moses — guitar
Spike Edney — keyboards
Neil Murray — bass
Cathy Porter – backing vocals
Shelley Preston – backing vocals
Cozy Powell – drums

Peter Green Splinter Group
Peter Green – guitars, vocals
Nigel Watson – guitars, vocals
Neil Murray – bass guitar
Spike Edney – keyboards
Cozy Powell – drums

Yngwie Malmsteen
Yngwie Malmsteen – guitar, bass, backing vocals
Mats Levén – lead vocals
Mats Olausson – keyboards
Barry Dunaway – bass
Cozy Powell – drums

Cozy Powell's Hammer
Gary Moore – guitar
Clem Clempson – guitar
Bernie Marsden – guitar
Jack Bruce – bass
Don Airey – keyboards
Max Middleton – keyboards
Cozy Powell – drums

Elmer Gantry – vocals
Frank Aiello – vocals
Kirby Gregory – guitar
Bernie Marsden – guitar
Jeff Beck – guitar
Gary Moore – guitar
Chris Glen – bass guitar
Neil Murray – bass guitar

Jack Bruce – bass guitar
John Cook – keyboards
Don Airey – keyboards
Mel Collins – saxophone
David Sancious – synth
Cozy Powell – drums

Colin Hodgkinson – bass guitar
Mel Galley – guitar
Gary Moore – guitar
Jon Lord – keyboards
Don Airey – keyboards
Cozy Powell – drums

Gerry Lane – vocals
Brian May –guitar
Jamie Page – guitar
Steve Lukather – guitar
Ray Fenwick – guitar, keyboards
Steve Makin – guitar, bass
Billy Sheehan – bass
John Deacon – bass
Laurence Cottle – bass
Neil Murray – bass
Don Airey – keyboards
Geoff Nichols – keyboards
John Sinclair – keyboards
Jon Lord – organ
Jeff Francis – synth
Cozy Powell – drums

John West – vocals
Mike Casswell – guitar
Sylvain – guitar
Neil Murray – bass
Ken Boley – keyboards
Lonnie Parks – keyboards
Viracocha – synth
Mike Burns – synth
Cozy Powell – drums

Appendices

DISCOGRAPHY

This discography is a basic listing of all the albums that Cozy is known to have appeared on. In the case of recordings under his own name, as well as his sixties bands, singles are also included, but to have included singles by all the other acts was outside the remit of this listing. Nor does the discography list numerous reissues or compliations from the artists of which there are many.

Albums
Over The Top (1979)
Tilt (1981)
Octopuss (1983)
The Drums Are Back (1992)
Especially For You (1999)

Singles
Dance With The Devil / And Then There Was Skin (1973)
The Man In Black / After Dark (1974)
Na Na Na / Mistral (1974)
Theme One / Over The Top (1979)
The Loner / El Sid (1979)
Heidi Goes To Town / Over The Top, Part 2 (1980)
Sooner Or Later / The Blister (1981)
Compilations
The Best of Cozy Powell (1997)

With The Sorcerers
Sweet Love / With You (1966)
Love Is A Beautiful Thing / Amen (1967)
Baby Lass Uns Tanzen Gehn / I Love A Girl From Heidelberg (1967)

With Young Blood
Green Light / Don't Leave Me In The Dark (1968)
Just How Loud / Masquerade (1968)
Bang-Shang-A-Lang / I Can't Stop (1968)
The Continuing Story Of Bungalow Bill / I Will (1969)

With Big Bertha
Live in Hamburg 1970 (2004)

With The Jeff Beck Group
Rough And Ready (1971)
Jeff Beck Group (1972)

With Bedlam
Bedlam (1973)
Anthology (2CD) (1999)
Live in London 1973 (2003)

With Rainbow
Rising (1976)
On Stage (1977)
Long Live Rock 'n' Roll (1978)
Down To Earth (1979)
Finyl Vinyl (1986)
Live in Germany 1976 (1990)
Live in Munich 1977 (2006)
Deutschland Tournee 1976 (2006)

With The Michael Schenker Group
MSG (1981)
One Night at Budokan (1982)

With Whitesnake
Slide It In (1984)
Live In 1984: Back To The Bone (2014)
With Emerson, Lake & Powell
Emerson, Lake & Powell (1986)
The Sprocket Sessions (2003)
Live in Concert (2003)

With Forcefield
Forcefield (1987)
Forcefield II: The Talisman (1988)
Forcefield III: To Oz And Back (1989)
Forcefield IV: Let The Wild Run Free (1991)
Instrumentals (1992)

Appendices

With Black Sabbath
Headless Cross (1989)
Tyr (1990)
Forbidden (1995)

With Brian May
Back To The Light (1992)
Live at The Brixton Academy (1994)
Another World (1998)
Red Special (1998)

Guest appearances and sessions
Tony Joe White – Swamp Music:
The Complete Monument Recordings – Live at the Isle of Wight
Festival 1970 (2006)
Ed Welch – Clowns (1971)
Harvey Andrews – Writer of Songs (1972)
Julie Felix – Clotho's Web (1972)
Donovan – Cosmic Wheels (1973)
Chick Churchill – You and Me (1973)
Murray Head – Nigel Lived (1973)
Tony Ashton and Jon Lord – First of the Big Bands (1974)
Bob Sargeant – The First Starring Role (1974)
Peter Sarstedt – Every Word You Say (1975)
Various – Peter & The Wolf (1976)
Hot Chocolate – XIV Greatest Hits (1976)
Bernie Marsden – And About Time Too! (1979)
Bernie Marsden – Look at Me Now (1981)
Graham Bonnet – Line-Up (1981)
The Young And Moody Band – Don't Do That / How Can I Help
You Tonight (1981)
Jon Lord – Before I Forget (1982)
Robert Plant – Pictures at Eleven (1982)
Phenomena – Phenomena (1985)
Roger Daltrey – Under a Raging Moon (1985)
Boys Don't Cry – Who the Am Dam do You Think We Am (1987)
Sanne Salomonsen – Ingen Engel (Danish Version) / No Angel
(English Version) (1987)

Warlock – Triumph and Agony (1987)
Pete York – Super Drumming Vol. 1 (1987)
Cinderella – Long Cold Winter (1988)
James Darby – Southern Region Breakdown (1988)
Don Airey – K2– Tales of Triumph and Tragedy (1988)
Gary Moore – After the War (1989)
Minute By Minute – Timewatch (1989)
Ritchie Blackmore – Rock Profile Vol. 2 (1991)
Various Artists – In From The Storm – The Music of Jimi Hendrix (1995)
Glenn Tipton – Baptizm of Fire (1997)
Peter Green Splinter Group – Peter Green Splinter Group (1997)
S.A.S. Band – SAS Band (1997)
Yngwie Malmsteen – Facing the Animal (1997)
Colin Blunstone – The Light Inside (1998)
Ace Kefford – Ace The Face (2003)
Tony Martin – Scream (2005)
Tipton, Entwistle & Powell – Edge of the World (2006)
Pete York – Super Drumming Vol. 3 (2008)

About The Author

Laura Shenton MA LLCM DipRSL has been thinking about music since she first heard it, possibly whilst still in the womb. She has a Masters degree in "Music Since 1900" from Liverpool Hope University. Her hobbies and interests include writing, playing the piano, staying up into the small hours wondering about life whilst eating crisps and obsessing about music, hamsters and dogs. In particular, her writing buddy is the best dog in the world — a black Labrador.

CPSIA information can be obtained
at www.ICGtesting.com
Printed in the USA
BVHW040247131121
621483BV00005B/258